Wileman
A Collectors Guide

by
Richard Knight
and
Susan Hill

Jazz Publications

Published in 1995 by

Jazz Publications Limited
45A Rother Street
Stratford Upon Avon
Warwickshire
CV37 6LT

Telephone : 01789 298362

Copyright Richard Knight, Susan Hill and Jazz Publications Limited

ISBN 0 9516525 3 2

All rights reserved. No part of this publication may be reproduced, stored in a retrieval system or transmitted in any form or by any means, electronic, mechanical, photocopying, recording or otherwise without the prior permission of Jazz Publications Limited.

Printed in England by Warwick Printing Company Limited

Contents

The Foley Potteries 1

China 1882 to 1910 7

Earthenware Ranges 51

Appendix A : Bibliography 89

Appendix B : Backstamps 90

Appendix C : Registered Numbers 93

Appendix D : China Reference Guide 94

Appendix E : Earthenware Reference Guide 135

Acknowledgements

Extracts from Pattern Books reproduced with the kind permission of the copyright owner and registered proprietor of the Shelley trade mark, Royal Doulton Limited. This book has been produced independently and neither the authors nor the publisher has any connection whatsoever with Royal Doulton Limited.

The items that appear in the book were photographed by courtesy of :

A J Partners, Manny Banner, John Barter, Allan Bellamy, Beverley & Beth Adams, Linda Ellis, Avice & Bryan Goodlad, Beth Hardcastle, Richard & Patricia Knight, Liz & Rhodri Lewis, Susan & David Pickles, Marcus Shelley, Vivian & Martin Truran, John & Joan Walton.

The valuable assistance of Alan Shelley, Valerie Shelley, Alexander Clement and the staff of Royal Doulton is gratefully acknowledged.

The additional details of registered numbers provided by Dr Anthony Russell-Jones was much appreciated.

Photography

Photographs of Pattern Books by Northern Counties Photographers, Burslem.
All other photographs by Rod Fawkes Photography, Cwmbran for Jazz Publications Ltd.

Important Note

Every effort has been made to provide accurate and comprehensive information. However, due to the incompleteness of the source material, inaccuracies and omissions have inevitably been made. The authors and publisher will not be held responsible for any losses incurred because of the information contained in this book. Any readers who wish to offer further information are invited to write to the authors via the publisher's address.

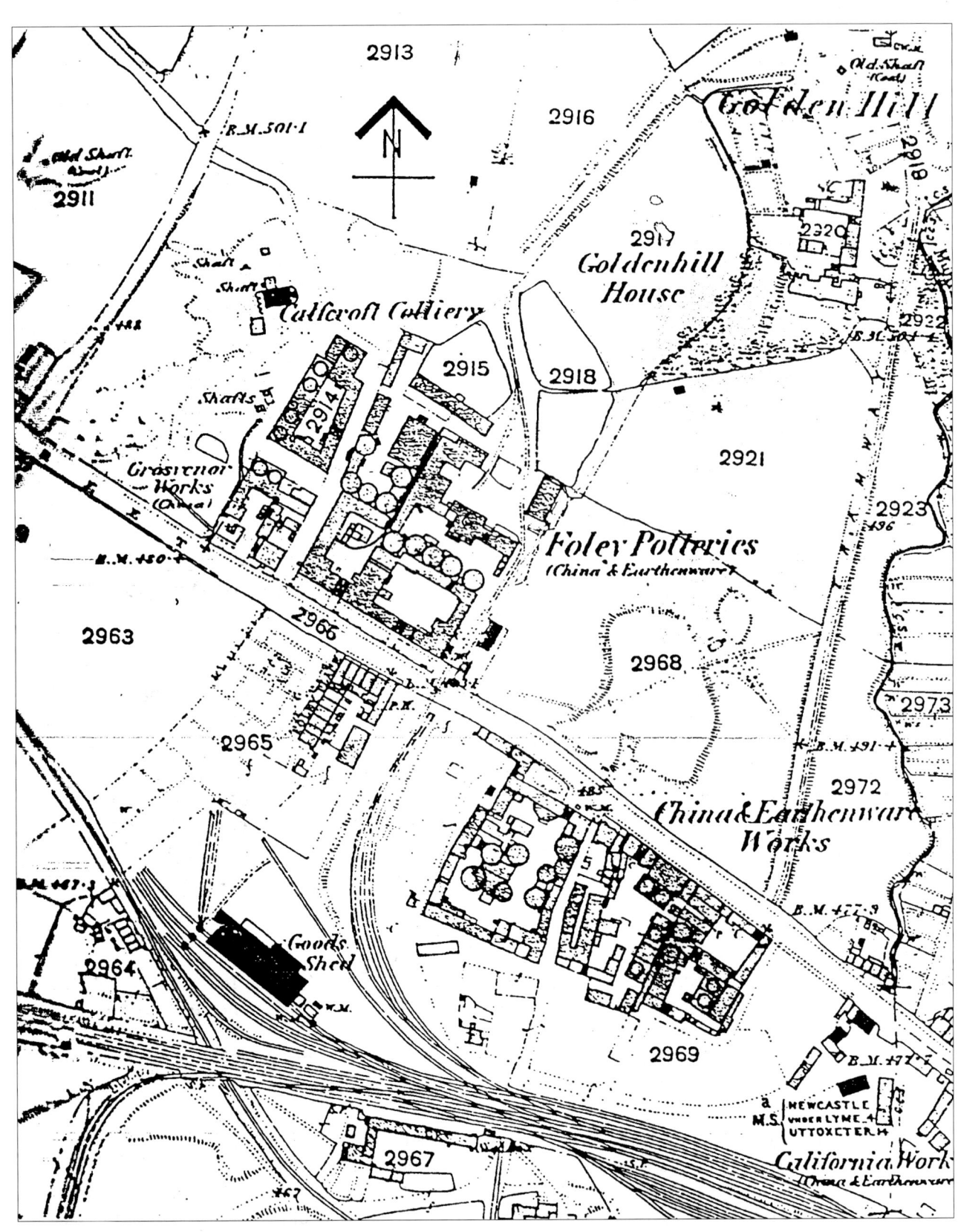

Extract from an Ordnance Survey Map (1877) showing The Foley Potteries and Foley China Works (Building 2914) situated along the north side of King Street

The Foley Potteries

The name Foley was derived from Foley House which was situated just south of King Street, between the districts of Fenton and Longton. It became associated with an area encompassing several potteries along the east part of King Street. Confusingly, each of these bore the name, Foley, and many incorporated "Foley" into their trademarks. These included the "Foley Pottery" operated by Barkers & Kent, the "Old Foley Pottery" of James Kent, E. Brain's "The Foley", and the Wileman potteries.

The history of the Foley china and earthenware works with which the Wileman and, later, the Shelley families were associated spans some 150 years. These works played an important part in the development of the pottery industry of Fenton. Founded around 1827, the "Foley Potteries" as it became known, developed from one of the many earthenware producers of the early to mid 19th century into an important manufacturer of china and ornamental earthenware known for its quality and design.

The original pottery was built by John Smith, a local landowner of Great Fenton Hall, whose family had owned a large part of Fenton for the past century. Built on an undeveloped area on the north side of King Street, the site provided both coal and clay, a good location for the delivery of materials and dispatch of ware, and space for future development.

The factory, built of brick and stone dressing, was set around a rectangular courtyard with the impressive facade of its long frontage reflecting the social prestige of its patron. Set back from the road the facade comprised an arched, key-stoned coach entrance to the factory with a central venetian window above and windows set in six bays to each side. The interior of some of the front rooms, used for offices and display, were given plastered walls and covered ceilings. By contrast to the front buildings, the working areas inside the courtyard were plain two storey buildings with no decorative features, smaller windows and outside staircases for access between floors. The five bottle ovens stood behind the main courtyard with covered walkways linking them with the rear workshops. At the time, it was regarded as a modern works also having a steam powered flint mill at the rear of the site.

Originally the factory was let to Thomas and George Elkin, John King Knight and John Bridgewood and produced ware under the trademarks K E & B and K E B. Thomas Elkin withdrew in 1833 and the others continued *"as makers of earthenware, dealers in china, colour grinders and farmers"*. Following the retirement of John Bridgewood in 1840, the business traded as Elkin, Knight & Co or sometimes as Knight, Elkin & Knight or Knight, Elkin & Co. After George Elkin's retirement in 1847, J K Knight continued alone.

During this early period blue-printed earthenware was produced including Willow and Broseley patterns. The proprietors soon established their reputation, being referred to as *"gentlemen of the most reliable character as tradesmen and members of civil society"*, and their pots as having *"attained celebrity in the markets"*. The factory itself came under the scrutiny of the Children's Employment Commissioner in 1841 and was reported to be *"modern, well constructed, open, roomy and in all respects good"*. It was probably much better than many of its contemporaries, although by later standards it had poor lighting, no ventilation, open fire heating in the rooms, no proper facilities and the workers were exposed to the extremes of temperature inherent in all potteries.

Reflecting the success of the business, further buildings were erected between 1832 and 1849 on the western side of the factory. The front of the new buildings, also facing King Street, were designed as a continuation of the earlier works with a similar facade and its own coaching entrance. The fittings in the new part were even more decorative than those of the earlier front rooms.

In 1853 J K Knight brought Henry Wileman into the business as a partner. Henry Wileman was a wholesale glass and Staffordshire ware dealer with premises in Paddington, London together with a china warehouse on the Edgeware Road. He was also the owner of the Church Gresley Pottery in Derbyshire which he retained until his death. Wileman's entry into the business probably reflected the need for increased capital at a time when more mechanical processes were being introduced into the industry. The partnership continued for three years, trading as Knight and Wileman, until in 1856, Knight retired and Henry Wileman took over the business trading under his own name.

The business, which by now employed around 220 workers, continued to expand and in 1860, Henry Wileman constructed a separate china works alongside the older buildings. The new works, known as the "Foley China Works" comprised a single quadrangle of three storey buildings set back from the main road and five bottle ovens. The map illustrates the layout of the Foley Potteries and the new china works (identified by reference 2914). It also shows the factory connected to the main goods railway by a private line leading to the rear of the works.

Following Henry Wileman's death in 1864, his two sons James and Charles took over the business trading as J & C Wileman. However, in 1866 the partnership was dissolved with Charles taking over the china works and James the earthenware works. On Charles' retirement in 1870, James became sole proprietor trading under his own name.

A landmark was reached in 1872 when James Wileman took into partnership Joseph Ball Shelley, who had joined the business as a traveller in 1862. The partnership was for the Foley China Works only (trading as Wileman & Co) and James Wileman continued to operate the earthenware works under his own name. In 1884, the partnership was dissolved when James Wileman retired from the china works leaving them to be run by Joseph Shelley who by then had been joined by his son Percy.

Joseph Shelley was born in January 1836 and brought up in Longton. He was the only son of Thomas Bolton Shelley whose family had been associated with the pottery industry in Lane End since the middle of the 18th century. His grandfather, also named Thomas, had been a potter at Lane Delph, situated only a few miles west of the Foley. Joseph became involved in the pottery industry through his step-father's partnership in the pottery firm of Hartshorn, Ferneyhough & Adams at the Dresden Works in Stafford Street, Longton. Originally an attorney's clerk, Joseph joined his stepfather in the business and, by 1858, had become a partner trading as Shelley & Hartshorn. The partnership was dissolved in 1861 and Joseph subsequently went into partnership with James and Harvey Adams, trading under the name of Shelley & Adams. This partnership was dissolved in March 1862 when Joseph joined Henry Wileman.

Percy Shelley was born in Longton in April 1860. After a boarding school education he went on to Owen's College, Manchester, obtaining a BA degree from London University. In 1881 he joined his father at Wileman & Co. Although without formal training, Percy was keen to improve the quality of the ware and standard of decoration not only at Wileman but within the industry as a whole. One example of his approach was the controversial and unpopular suggestion that German potters should be invited to set up a factory in Longton to teach local manufacturers better techniques.

He also played an active role in local community affairs being President of the North Staffordshire Liberal Party, a magistrate, and a key figure in the North Staffordshire Chamber of Commerce. Percy was a well known and respected figure in the pottery industry, typical of the family businessmen of his time. Strong willed and a strict employer, he was also a campaigner for his industry and the people employed by it. He remained with the firm for some 50 years, until his retirement in 1932.

The business thrived during the 1880s with a report in June 1889 noting that *"Messrs Shelley & Co of the Foley Works, Longton are enlarging and making extensive alterations to their works"*. A bridge was built linking the old Foley Potteries and the new china works.

In 1892, James Wileman retired and the original earthenware works were closed. The contents were sold by auction over three days and included *"valuable potters utensils, material stores, including about four tons of copper plates, many of them being good going patterns amongst which are 'Rustic', 'Fairy', 'Formosa', 'Springtime', 'Aldersgate', 'French', 'Nyanza', 'Palm', 'Clematis', 'Lake Scenery', 'Cashmere', 'Passion Flower', 'Wynthrop', 'Seasons'."*

A report in the trade journal at the time bitterly reflected on the impact of the closure, *"Monday, the 31st, sees the beginning of the sale of Messrs Wileman's works, at Fenton, and it is safe to prophesy that manufacturers in the same line of business with any money to spend will be there. Mr Wileman is one of those who find no inducement to stay in the business, and he is presumably able to do without it, he has decided to deliver himself from the cares and ties of a large and intricate business. This is all very well, but it is no doubt hard upon the work-people, who are mostly not able to do without it, and will not too easily find employment elsewhere."*

These works were partly occupied by J Goodwin, Stoddard & Co and McKee & Sons around the turn of the century and continued to be let until their demolition in 1984, the last occupant being China & Earthenware Millers Ltd.

The difficult economic situation of the 1890s impacted on the pottery trade although Wileman & Co seem not to have been affected significantly. This is highlighted by a report in the Pottery Gazette of September 1893 which stated : *"The old name of Wileman seems destined to enjoy a long lease of life, judging from the energetic manner in which the manufactory is now being carried on by the present proprietor; Mr Shelley, and by his son, Mr Percy Shelley, who, indeed, have had the business for many years. We found it quite a relief from the continuous complaints of the depression in the china trade (perhaps this particular line has suffered more than any other in the pottery industry) to find a few firms who have kept briskly at work as Messrs Wileman have done, for within the last few years they have been continually enlarging their works, so that at the present time its capacity for turning out china has been quite doubled, and even now plans are being prepared for important additions to cope with the increased development of their trade with the Colonies and the United States, whither they send a representative at stated intervals."*

In 1893 Percy Shelley visited the Chicago exhibition to study the American market, bringing home ideas which boosted the firm's export trade. To facilitate the increased business, showrooms were opened in Holborn, London for both home and foreign trade, and agents appointed in Australia and North America.

Around 1894, Wileman & Co built a new earthenware works together with new offices, showrooms and warehouses, all in the three storey style. These new works, used to produce ornamental earthenware, were situated on recently acquired land to the west of the Foley China Works.

On the death of Joseph Shelley in 1896, Percy Shelley became the sole proprietor of the business. The policy of improving the quality, design and decoration of the ware had begun a few years earlier with the employment of artists under Micklewright and the engagement of Rowland Morris, a ceramic modeller and designer. It continued with the appointment, in 1896, of Frederick Rhead as Art Director. The choice of Rhead again demonstrated Percy Shelley's ability to gather craftsmen around him. Equally important, the two men had a common philosophy in their desire to promote good artistry and design within a commercial environment.

It is worth reviewing Rhead's career prior to joining Wileman. He was born into a family of artists and designers with his father, grandfather and great-uncles all being significantly associated with the pottery industry. Frederick continued the tradition by becoming a student at art school where he won a number of national medals and prizes for ceramic art. In 1872, he joined Minton where he worked as an apprentice under Louis Solon, gaining experience of the pate-sur-pate decorating technique. From Minton, he joined Josiah Wedgwood where he was employed until 1883.

After leaving Wedgwood, he became Art Director at a series of potteries, namely James Gildea, E.J.D. Bodley, and the Brownfields Pottery. Hence, by the time he joined Wileman, Rhead had experience of a wide range of techniques and had worked alongside some of the most noted designers and artists of the late nineteenth century. Rhead had a profound influence on the design of both china and earthenware during his nine years with Wileman & Co, and was particularly noted for the innovative earthenware produced.

By the turn of the century the combined china and earthenware works had achieved the basic layout it was to maintain. Working conditions were still in need of improvement despite developments in industrial practices. Industrial illnesses, including lead poisoning and lung diseases, were still common and Percy Shelley was active in campaigning for better conditions in the industry and compensation for its workers.

In 1899 the firm was reported in "The Artist" to be employing *"two hundred lady and girl artists and a score or so of male designers .... the designs are mainly due to the taste and enterprise of Mr Percy Shelley, the proprietor of the firm, aided by Messrs Rhead, Stephen Hartly, Banks, Wood and Forester, the Misses Robinson, Price, Brown and others. Designs have been supplied by the late Rowland Morris, P G Riley, Miss Waterhouse and many other well known artists"*.

In 1905 Frederick Rhead was succeeded as Art Director by Walter Slater. The Slater family also had a long tradition of artistic achievement within the ceramic industry working for such factories as Derby and Minton. Walter trained at Mintons and then worked under his uncle, John Slater, at Doulton & Co in Burslem where he established his reputation as a designer and potter. The weakening of demand for china and ornamental ware during Walter Slater's first five years with Wileman & Co limited his scope for displaying the full range of his talent. However, after about 1910 he made a major contribution to the development of very successful ornamental pottery and earthenware, and fine china.

Although a member of the Shelley family had been proprietor of the china business since 1884 the company continued to trade as Wileman & Co. In 1910 Percy Shelley attempted to register Foley China as a tradename. However, E. Brain & Co, who also used the Foley name, objected. Following a court ruling that Wileman & Co could make no exclusive claim to the name, the company adopted Shelley as its tradename. For the first few years the words "Late Foley" were incorporated into the Shelley trademark. The change was accompanied with the announcement that *"The world-wide reputation of 'Foley' China has caused many cheap imitations and in future, to protect the public, the real and genuine 'Foley' china will always be indelibly marked 'Shelley China', a trademark which is the guarantee of the highest excellence."*

The business continued in the Shelley family with Percy Shelley's sons. Percy Norman and Vincent Bob first joined in 1913, and returned after the war, and Kenneth Jack joined from university in 1919. Norman was responsible for the production side of the business, with Bob taking over the warehouses and stock control and Jack the finances. In 1925 the registered name of the company was changed from Wileman & Co to "Shelleys" with the announcement *"There is no useful purpose served by using the name Wileman any longer"*. In 1929 it became the limited company of Shelley Potteries.

In 1920, a new office block and showroom were built on the site between the new china and earthenware works and King Street, to the west of the Grosvenor Works. The new showroom was

China scouring at Wileman & Co China Works showing the mechanical ventilation system for extraction of dust. (Published in HM Inspector of Factories Annual Report 1899)

A factory view of Wileman & Co showing the new works linked to the older buildings (far right) by a bridge

described in 1925 as one of the best appointed in the Potteries. Further improvements were made to the layout of the works to improve their efficiency.

Walter Slater retired in 1937 and was succeeded as Art Director by his son, Eric, who had joined the firm in 1919.

The Second World War led to the direct involvement of the government in the pottery industry. A number of measures were introduced in an attempt to balance the need to release labour for munition work with the preservation of revenue from the export trade. Quota systems were applied which resulted in the majority of decorated wares being assigned for export only. In addition, the Concentration Scheme of 1941 aimed to concentrate production in as few factories as possible so that those factories remaining in business worked to full capacity. Shelley's obtained the necessary certificate and remained open, taking over the production of Jackson and Gosling, whose Grosvenor Works were adjacent.

During the war, plans were made for a major reorganisation of the factory and in 1945 the decision was made to discontinue earthenware manufacture. In that year, Bob Shelley died and his two sons, Alan and Donald, joined the company as Sales Director and Technical Director respectively, bringing a fourth generation of the Shelley family into the business.

The earthenware and china factories were combined, with the Foley China Works becoming potters shops and the earthenware factory being converted into decorating shops and warehouses. Electric kilns and glost ovens began replacing the bottle ovens in the post war period with 'Top Hat' kilns, designed by Donald Shelley, being introduced in the mid 1950s. By 1957 the last of the bottle ovens had been demolished.

Donald's interest and expertise in kiln manufacture led to a business diversification with the formation of Shelley Electric Furnaces Ltd in May 1956. In addition to meeting the requirements of the Shelley factory, this company aimed to manufacture and sell kilns to other potteries. Construction facilities were located on adjacent land purchased from Jackson and Gosling in 1953.

In 1965 Shelley Potteries were renamed Shelley China Limited, and the following year the company was taken over by Allied English Potteries. The china works was renamed Montrose Works and was used for the production of Royal Albert bone china. In 1971 the company became part of the Doulton Group. Today only the 1920s office and showroom block remains, a part of which is used by the Sir Henry Doulton School of Sculpture; a fitting use for the last vestige of a pottery with such a history of innovation and design.

China 1882 to 1910

When Percy Shelley joined his father Joseph Shelley, in 1881, he was keen to improve the china produced by Wileman & Co which Jewitt had described as being *"of the ordinary useful class for household purposes"*. Although produced for both home and export trade, the china was not of a particularly high quality the wares being plain white or with line borders of printed decoration. It is not known precisely which teaware ranges were produced at this time as the earliest surviving pattern book (begun circa 1882) does not record the shapes for many of the early pattern numbers. However, Victoria, Worcester and Minton can be identified from around 1882 and are likely to have been in production from an earlier date. Similarly, pattern descriptions make reference to pre-1882 pattern numbers.

In 1884, the introduction of an octagonal shape known as Square or Queen Anne was a significant step in the development of Wileman teaware. This innovative shape was the first from the company to be registered under the Patents, Designs and Trade Marks Act of 1883 (number 6559). Although only in production for a few years, it was to form the basis for the elegant Antique shape (1905) and the very successful later Queen Anne range (1926).

1886 saw further significant changes with the registration of the Albert and Alexandra ranges. Albert was originally known as Jubilee Flute, presumably to commemorate Queen Victoria's Golden Jubilee of 1887, and would appear to be a ribbed development of the traditional Victoria shape with a handle identical to the Square range. Alexandra, described as Square Fluted for the first twelve pattern numbers, was developed from the Square shape and, like Albert, was ribbed. The Alexandra shape continued the move away from Wileman's more traditional cup design and was produced with a substantial number of patterns.

Under Percy Shelley's influence there was a marked improvement in the quality of the wares and by the late 1880's further major shapes had been introduced namely Lily, Fairy and Daisy. Around 1891, the Shell shape, with its highly sculptured appearance, added further variety to the range of teaware produced.

The decorations applied to the teaware were principally plain or shaded colours or single colour transfer prints. The prints varied from simple floral or ornamental border designs to elaborate patterns covering most of the ware. Many were available in a variety of colours such as the widely used Ivy pattern which was produced in seventeen individual plain colours and many shaded variations. Many transfer patterns were applied across the major ranges in production and their use reflected the improvements which had been achieved in transfer printing techniques. A small number of patterns were also extended by employing the print and enamel method of decoration which used a background transfer enhanced by hand painting. The exceptions to the generally simple colour printed designs included the Japan patterns (discussed further below) which involved hand painting and gilding over a transfer design normally printed in red.

By the early 1890s, with the extension of the china factory and the need to meet the demands of the export trade, Percy Shelley was looking to further improve the quality and design of both china and its decoration. With the potential American export markets in mind, he engaged a number of artists under Micklewright who were notable for their poultry, fish, game and landscape subjects. The factory continued to produce painted centres to plates past the turn of the century with Micklewright, Alcock, Mussell and Hewitt still being recorded against dessert plate pattern numbers around 1903/4.

January 1, 1898. THE POTTERY GAZETTE.

AMERICAN BUYERS SHOULD CALL AND SEE OUR NEW LINES.

WILEMAN & CO.,

MANUFACTURERS OF

ART PORCELAIN

FOR

THE HOME TRADE,
AMERICA,
AUSTRALASIA, & the COLONIES.

WORKS—

The Foley Potteries, Longton.

London Show Rooms—26, THAVIES INN, HOLBORN CIRCUS.

REPRESENTATIVES—

Home Trade—Mr. C. APPLETON and Mr.
United States America and Canada—Mr. G. H. SHUBOTHAM.
Australasia—Mr. NEALE HARRISON, Melbourne.

CONSTANT SUPPLY OF NOVELTIES FOR AMERICA.

HOTEL CHINA.

DOMESTIC AND ARTISTIC CHINA OF FINEST GRADE.

TABLE DECORATIONS and FANCY GOODS of all DESCRIPTIONS.

PRICE LISTS ON APPLICATION.

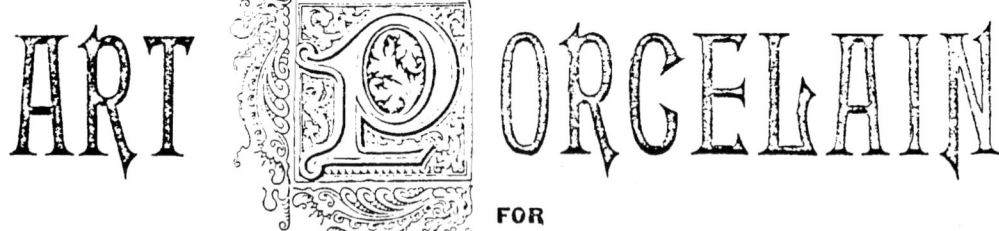

Advertisement from the Pottery Gazette, 1898

By 1893 the factory was producing a wide range of services : teasets, breakfast sets, coffee sets, five o'clock sets, solitaire sets and dessert ware. That year saw the introduction of a further major range, the delicately scalloped Empire shape, possibly developed from the Daisy range, which was well received by the trade. A report in September 1893 noted *"We were much pleased with the general artistic excellence of the Foley Works China. For many years this firm have been noted for the first-class quality of their ordinary bulk china; latterly they have made a special effort to cater for the taste which has sprung up for high-class china. In tea and breakfast china, besides familiar patterns we noticed many others of sterling merit, their new "Empire" shape being one of the best we have seen for some time. We certainly think that our American cousins will fall in love with it. The patterns it has been done in are very rich and varied, showing that much thoughtful care has been exercised in their selection, the colours employed being exceptionally good."* The report went on to comment on the great number of patterns and shapes of five o'clock sets and the attention that had been paid to the modelling and decoration of solitaire sets. It describes the new shape as especially graceful in dessert ware with the flowers and landscapes beautifully painted. It concludes that *"There is a spirit displayed which entirely disposes of the idea that English manufacturers were behind the times."*

The succesful Foley shape was introduced in 1894 followed by the Century shape. In 1896 the company registered and introduced an important new range, Dainty, with fluted panels and scalloped edges. Designed by Rowland Morris, this range was produced to a higher quality than some earlier ranges. It proved very successful, particularly for export to the United States, Canada and Australia and continued in production until 1966. The early wares were plain white or in shaded colours but later floral designs were applied. The shape was also used extensively for crested ware.

A further range, called Snowdrop, was also registered and introduced in 1896. Like Daisy and Empire this too was of scalloped design. With rather more sweeping lines to the cup, the style was appropriate to the late 1890s and was produced with patterns ranging from delicate transfer prints to bolder Art Nouveau designs.

The appointment of Frederick Rhead as Art Director in 1896 was a significant turning point for Wileman & Co. Although primarily known for his work on earthenware, he had a substantial influence on china designs, both for teaware including painted centres for dessert plates, and a variety of china items such as lamps, flowerpots and beer pulls.

Under Rhead's influence the quality of the designs continued to improve reflecting the company's aim of producing daintier china. Examples of the elegant shapes introduced during his period as Art Director include the very successful Gainsborough (and the Milton variant) around the turn of the century; Royal, around 1902; and Antique and Court, both of which were registered in December 1904. The patterns also reflected his more ambitious approach, both in design and the use of colour, particularly during the latter stage of his time with the company.

A particularly innovative range of teaware known as Edward was introduced in 1905 but was in production for a very short period. It was unlike any earlier - or indeed later - ranges in that the fine china had an apple blossom design which was moulded and then painted.

Around the turn of the century, Wileman began to diversify into other areas of china production. In 1899, a range of miniature items, Gems, was introduced which included cups and saucers, and vases. Nursery ware was introduced in 1902 with the early designs being simple lithograph illustrations of popular nursery rhymes. Since the 1880's, Wileman had produced badged china for commercial use, for example by hotels, and had begun producing commemorative ware for Queen Victoria's Golden Jubilee in 1887 with subsequent major events being recognised.However, in the early 1900's crested china became particularly popular and many heraldic designs were applied to both miniature items and teaware, providing a useful source of business during a depressed time in the industry.

In 1905 Frederick Rhead left and was replaced as Art Director by Walter Slater, another designer of wide experience with Minton and Doulton. During his first few years with Wileman & Co the generally depressed state of the industry limited the opportunity for him to exercise his talents to the full, his major influence on teaware designs coming after 1910. Nevertheless, a few new ranges were introduced, such as Dorothy, and there was the development of the Lily shape to the Argyle (New Lily) and Low Lily ranges. The patterns up to 1910 continued to show the quality and design established under Rhead's direction, with lithographic transfers being used more frequently.

A selection of James Wileman earthenwares

Early shape ranges including Lily, Albert, Victoria and Worcester

Japan Patterns

Patterns adapted from 17th and early 18th century Imari designs became popular in the 19th century and were introduced by several china factories, including Derby and Wileman. Imari designs were originally brought to Europe on porcelain made in Arita, in the Hizen province of Japan, and exported via the port of Imari, hence their name. These early designs, which may originally have been influenced by Dutch traders, comprised a rich decoration of flowers and birds in red, blue and gold, and became known as "Old Japan". The Japan patterns which became popular in the 19th century retained the style and richness of the original Imari.

Japan patterns are recorded in the Wileman china pattern books from the early 1880s. They involve transfer prints in red, generally of a floral design, with hand painting in black, blue or darker red around the print, and gilding of the borders of the design or sometimes overlaying the painted areas of the pattern.

The first design to be registered by Wileman & Co under the Patents, Designs and Trade Marks Act of 1883 was in fact a Japan pattern; registration number 3931 (March 1884). This particular design proved to be very successful being applied to many teaware ranges and continuing in use beyond 1910.

In all approximately 40 different Japan designs making up some 100 patterns were applied to most of Wileman's major teaware ranges. With a few exceptions the Japan designs occurred before 1895 with the major ones being registered.

Square/Queen Anne teaset with Japan pattern (3476), the first pattern applied to this shape

Examples of Japan patterns

Japan patterns including Rd Number 3931 (top), the first registration by Wileman under the 1883 Act, shown on the Victoria, Worcester, Foley and Dorothy shapes

A selection of Japan patterns

Alexandra shape teaset with Clover print pattern enhanced by enamelling

Teawares of various shapes illustrating the print and enamel method of decoration

17

Examples of the Alexandra shape

Summary of Shapes

The details of Wileman teaware included in this chapter are derived from the original pattern books which formed the working documents of the factory. They cover the period from 1882, the date of the earliest surviving pattern book, to 1910.

The teaware shapes produced during this period have been identified and, in most cases, illustrated, with dates given where possible. These dates have been derived from the pattern numbers for a particular shape and as such can only provide a guide to the length of time a particular shape was in production. The total number of patterns is based on the patterns originally designated to that shape in the pattern books. However, some patterns were applied to other shapes not recorded in the pattern books. The pattern number is normally hand painted on the base of particular teaware items.

The sequence of china pattern numbers can be rather confusing. A new series of numbers starting at 6002 was introduced around 1890 possibly the result of the major changes to the china works at this time. This operated concurrent with the original series (3348 to 6001 and 9002 to 10548) until January 1911 when the china pattern books were amalgamated. They were further rationalised in 1919 with all numbers still in production being transferred to a new book. A schedule of the china pattern books is given at Appendix D to illustrate the chronology, followed by detailed lists of pattern numbers, grouped under their respective series with brief descriptions of the patterns.

From 1884, some new shapes and patterns were registered under the Patents, Designs and Trade Marks Act of 1883. Where it has been possible to identify registered numbers with particular shapes or pattern numbers they have been noted. A listing of registered numbers relating to Wileman is given in Appendix C.

A further guide to dating are the backstamps used by Wileman & Co although not all pieces will be found to have such markings. The backstamps, including those used subsequently by Shelley, are illustrated at Appendix B, the two important changes for Wileman & Co occurring around 1892 and 1910.

It is likely the 1892 change of trademark, incorporating the words "The Foley" and "The Foley China", was associated with Joseph Shelley becoming the sole proprietor of the Foley Potteries. The further change of trademark arose following the unsuccessful attempt in 1910 to register "Foley China" as a trade name. As a result the "Shelley" mark was introduced in 1910, incorporating the words "Late Foley" until 1916.

Figure 1 : Albert

Figure 2 : Alexandra

Figure 3 : Antique

Figure 4 : Argyle

ALBERT

First Pattern Number :	3632	Date :	1886
Last Pattern Number :	4010	Date :	1890
Number of Patterns :	39		

The Albert shape was registered in November 1886 (Number 60868). Introduced in December 1886, it was originally known as Jubilee Flute for 17 pattern numbers (3632 - 3641 and 3645 - 3651) before being called Albert.
See Figure 1.

ALEXANDRA (ALEX)

First Pattern Number :	3695	Date :	1887
Last Pattern Number :	9551	Date :	1902
Number of Patterns :	162		

The Alexandra shape, generally known as Alex, was registered in November 1886 (Number 60650). The shape was first described in the pattern books as Square Fluted and identified against numbers 3695 - 3706 although an annotation of 17 August 1887 indicates these were of "No 2 quality" and "not to be numbered". The last recorded pattern number is dated 1902 although examples of the shape have been found with a post 1910 Shelley backstamp. The few numbers between 1894 and 1902 all refer to special orders for badged ware.
See Figure 2.

ANTIQUE

| First Pattern Number : | 7843 | Date : | 1905 |
| Continued Post 1910 | | | |

The Antique shape was registered in December 1904 (Number 447136) and continued post 1910. When first introduced this octagonal shape was also described as Square and appears to have been based on the earlier Square (q.v.) (also known as Queen Anne) introduced in 1884 and for which the last pattern number was recorded in 1888. It formed the basis of a new Queen Anne shape introduced in 1926.
See Figure 3.

ARGYLE

| First Pattern Number : | 10471 | Date : | 1910 |
| Continued Post 1910 | | | |

Also described as New Lily.
See Figure 4.

21

Figure 5 : Bute

Figure 6 : Century

Figure 7 : Court

Figure 8 : Dainty

BUTE

First Pattern Number :   4071   Date :   1890
Continued Post 1910

The shape was first identified for patterns 4071 and 4072, as seconds for New Zealand, and did not arise again until pattern number 8017 in 1907.
See Figure 5.

CENTURY

First Pattern Number :   5622   Date :   1895
Last Pattern Number :   7320   Date :   1902
Number of Patterns :   122
See Figure 6.

COURT

First Pattern Number :   10051   Date :   1906
Continued Post 1910

Registered in December 1904 (Number 447137) with the last recorded pattern in 1913. The name was re-introduced in 1935 for a different shape.
See Figure 7.

DAINTY

First Pattern Number :   6858   Date :   1896
Continued Post 1910

Designed by Rowland Morris and registered in 1896 (Number 272101) Dainty proved to be a highly successful range, continuing in production until the Shelley factory closed in 1966.
See Figure 8.

DAISY

First Pattern Number :   3966   Date :   1889
Continued Post 1910

Registered in 1888 (Number 115510) with the last recorded pattern in 1913.
See Figure 9.

Figure 9 : Daisy

Figure 10 : Dorothy

Figure 11 : Edward

Figure 12 : Empire

DEVONSHIRE (DEVON)

First Pattern Number :   7851   Date : 1905
Last Pattern Number :   10090   Date : 1906
Number of Patterns :   28

Only 9 designs were applied to this shape. The name was re-introduced in 1937 for a different shape.

DOROTHY

First Pattern Number :   10169   Date : 1906
Continued Post 1910

See Figure 10.

EDWARD

First Pattern Number :   7871   Date : 1905
Last Pattern Number :   7878   Date : 1905
Number of Patterns :   8

Edward was a moulded design and the eight patterns refer to different colourways.
See Figure 11.

EMPIRE

First Pattern Number :   4971   Date : 1893
Last Pattern Number :   10449   Date : 1910
Number of Patterns :   192

Registered in 1893 (Number 108329). It is known that production continued post-1910. The name was re-introduced in 1930 but for a different shape.
See Figure 12.

FAIRY

First Pattern Number :   4131   Date : 1890
Last Pattern Number :   6827   Date : 1895
Number of Patterns :   216

Registered in July 1890 (Number 153594). Also described as New Fairy for a few patterns (9116-7 and 9131-9145). A deeper cup version was introduced as Violet (q.v.) in 1899.
See Figure 13.

FOLEY

First Pattern Number : 5211 Date : 1894
Last Pattern Number : 10441 Date : 1910
Number of Patterns : 175

See Figure 14.

FOLEY FLUTE

First Pattern Number : 7806 Date : 1904
Continued Post 1910

See Figure 15.

GAINSBOROUGH

First Pattern Number : 7072 Date : 1900
Continued Post 1910

Prior to 1910, Gainsborough was also used to describe a variant with a less pronounced foot. (See Milton).
See Figure 16.

GLADSTONE

First Pattern Number : 3583 Date : 1886
Continued Post 1910

The shape was used for special orders of badged ware, with the last recorded pattern in 1913.

LILY

First Pattern Number : 3818 Date : 1888
Continued Post 1910

Last recorded pattern in 1918.
See Figure 17.

(NEW) LOW LILY

First Pattern Number : 10167 Date : 1906
Continued Post 1910

Last recorded pattern in 1914.
See Figure 18.

A selection of patterns shown on the Snowdrop shape

Pages from the pattern book showing patterns for the Snowdrop shape

Pattern designs from the pattern book for the Square/Queen Anne shape

28

Evolution of a shape, from Square/Queen Anne (top) to Antique (centre) to the Queen Anne of the 1920s (bottom right)

Examples of the Shell and Dainty shapes

A selection of patterns applied to the Empire shape

Illustration of the Daisy shape including transfer printed and enamelled designs

Fairy and Violet shapes

Rococo dessert plate decorated by Micklewright

Two pages from the pattern book

MAY

First Pattern Number :	4689	Date :	1893
Last Pattern Number :	5305	Date :	1894
Number of Patterns :	70		

MILTON

First Pattern Number :   7447   Date :   1900
Continued Post 1910

A variant of Gainsborough (q.v.) with a less pronounced foot to the cup, this shape was only described as Milton post 1910
See Figure 19.

MINTON

First Pattern Number :	3417	Date :	c. 1883
Last Pattern Number :	10190	Date :	1907
Number of Patterns :	42		

Although the first recorded pattern is 3417, it is likely the shape was used for earlier unidentified patterns. It was used primarily for special orders of badged ware.

NEW YORK

First Pattern Number :   4073   Date :   1890
Continued Post 1910

The shape was first identified for patterns 4073 and 4074, as seconds for New Zealand, and did not arise again until pattern number 9231 in 1900.
See Figure 20.

PARIS

First Pattern Number :	3731	Date :	1887
Last Pattern Number :	5397	Date :	1895
Number of Patterns :	7		

The shape was used for a few special orders of badged ware.

Figure 13 : Fairy

Figure 14 : Foley

Figure 15 : Foley Flute

Figure 16 : Gainsborough

Figure 17 : Lily

Figure 18 : Low Lily

Figure 19 : Milton

Figure 20 : New York

Figure 21 : Royal

Figure 22 : Shell

Figure 23 : Snowdrop

POPPY

First Pattern Number : 6861 Date : 1895
Last Pattern Number : 6870 Date : 1895
Number of Patterns : 4

Only used for four patterns, the shape has a similar saucer to Dainty (q.v) whose introduction Poppy immediately preceded. It is therefore possible that this shape is closely associated with the introduction of Dainty.

ROMAN

First Pattern Number : 3601 Date : 1886
Continued Post 1910

The shape was used principally for special orders of badged ware, with the last recorded pattern in 1913.

ROYAL

First Pattern Number : 7462 Date : 1902
Continued Post 1910

Last recorded pattern in 1916.
See Figure 21.

SHELL

First Pattern Number : 4184 Date : 1891
Last Pattern Number : 5365 Date : 1894
Number of Patterns : 86

Registered in May 1890 (Number 150035).
See Figure 22.

SILVER

First Pattern Number : 3900 Date : 1889
Continued Post 1910

The shape was used for special orders of badged ware, with the last recorded pattern in 1917.

Figure 24 : Square

Figure 25 : Victoria

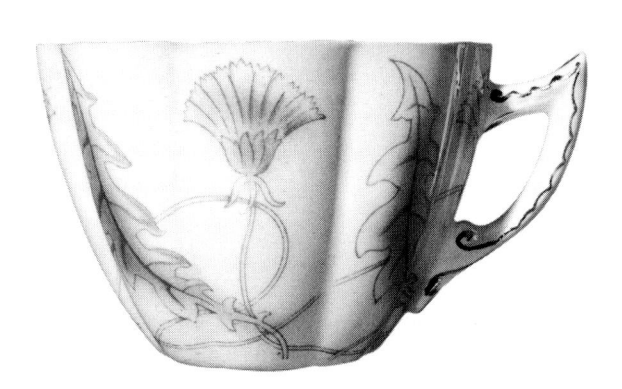

Figure 26 : Violet

Figure 27 : Worcester

SNOWDROP

First Pattern Number :   5721   Date :   1896
Continued Post 1910

Registered in 1896 (Number 272764), with the last recorded pattern in 1914.
See Figure 23.

SQUARE (QUEEN ANNE)

First Pattern Number :   3476   Date :   1884
Last Pattern Number :   3774   Date :   1888
Number of Patterns :   84

Square was registered in May 1884 (Number 6559). The octagonal shape was recorded as Square or Queen Anne (or sometimes both) and formed the basis of the later Antique (q.v.) shape which itself was described as Square for the first few patterns. The name Queen Anne was re-introduced in 1926 for a shape derived from Antique.
See Figure 24.

VICTORIA

First Pattern Number :   3412   Date :   1883
Continued Post 1910

Although the first recorded pattern is 3412, it is likely the shape was used for earlier unidentified patterns.
See Figure 25.

VIOLET

First Pattern Number :   9121   Date :   1899
Continued Post 1910

A deeper cup version of Fairy, also using the same registered number (153594). The pattern numbers continue to 1913.
See Figure 26.

WORCESTER

First Pattern Number :   3417   Date :   c. 1883
Continued Post 1910

Although the first recorded pattern is 3417, it is likely the shape was used for earlier unidentified patterns.
See Figure 27.

YORK

First Pattern Number :   5412   Date :   1895
Last Pattern Number :   10166   Date :   1906
Number of patterns   :   45

From 1905 the shape was described as Old York, presumably to distinquish it from the separate New York (q.v.) shape. The name York was re-introduced in 1932 for a different shape.

COFFEES

In addition to the coffee cups of many of the shapes listed above, other coffees identified are Stanley, Bamboo and Turkish cans.

Examples of the Royal, Gainsborough, Milton and Century shapes. NB The Ashbourne pattern shown on the Gainsborough breakfast cup (centre) is a post-1910 pattern

Number	Shape		
6906	Trinket Rococo.	Shaded Salmon from edge & Ivory in Centre. Whole of Houses painted on top (see 5832) in *Golden Green*. Sized Liquid Burnt edge. 1/9	
6907	Century	Surrey Scenery Painted in 62 Brown. Enamelled Fully. Burnished Handle only. White edge.	

Detailed design in the pattern book to be applied to the Century shape

44

A selection of New York, Low Lily, Dorothy, Argyle, Foley Flute and Bute shapes

A variety of shapes including Foley, Edward and Court

Nurserywares

Badged wares including town crests and advertising articles

Earthenware and china commemorative wares

A selection of earthenwares including a glazed parian flowerpot, Delphic and Moonlight patterns

Earthenware Ranges

The earliest earthenwares produced by Wileman were uninspiring and included printed and lustre decorations, 'shining blacks', cream coloured and granite wares. These were of ordinary quality for general household use with a considerable amount being exported to such markets as the United States, Australia, South Africa, Ceylon and India.

Two men were primarily responsible for elevating Wileman general earthenwares to the respected standard of 'Foley Art Pottery' - namely, Percy Shelley and Frederick Rhead.

Frederick Rhead's influence was felt in all areas of the company's product design. However, he was particularly responsible for a series of innovative earthenware ranges - Intarsio, Urbato, Spano-Lustra, Pastello and Primitif. It was these ranges that prompted the Artist periodical, in 1898, to state that : *"They have shown that it is possible to produce well-designed pottery, manufactured by legitimate methods and covered with beautiful glazes and enamels, at a price within the reach of the average citizen. They have had the courage to fling aside all the cherished traditions of the modern British potter, and have been rewarded by the instant approval of the buying public."*

Intarsio

Intarsio was the most popular and longest-lived of the ranges instigated by Rhead. Consequently, the largest number of designs were produced in this series, many of which were applied to only one shape.

The name was probably of Italian derivation although Rhead was also greatly influenced by the underglaze wares produced by the Dutch potteries, particularly Rozenburg.

Decorations were applied, prior to the glaze, by utilising an outline transfer of the pattern which was then fully handpainted, usually by the female decorating staff.

The patterns encompassed a wide range of styles and themes. These included various floral motifs; panels of animals, fish and birds; Egyptian and Red Indian characters. A Shakespearean series used scenes and text from the plays whilst famous politicians formed the basis for a range of character tea and coffee pots.

A considerable variety of shapes was also produced including vases, plaques, loving-cups, clock cases, umbrella stands and jardinieres with pedestals.

Urbato

The Urbato decorations were executed entirely by hand and were primarily a multicoloured adaptation of the traditional sgraffito technique.

The article, for example a vase, was usually made of a dark-toned clay which had one or more films of different coloured clay(s) on its surface onto which the pattern was sketched. The design was then scratched or incised with a steel tool through the film(s) to the darker coloured background.

The process was repeated, depending on the number of layers of film, with other colours being subsequently added with a brush if required.

Some designs within the Urbato range were based on tubelining, a method which used a technique similar to that of icing a cake. A bag containing liquid clay was squeezed through a narrow glass tube onto the article being decorated making a thin raised line. The pattern could be applied in various ways, for example the tube-liner could carry it out freehand following a model prepared by the designer or the pattern could be marked out in pencil on the article by the designer prior to the tube-liner commencing work.

The designs are predominantly stylised floral and plant motifs with some use of more abstract patterns. However, there are also repeating designs of monkeys, penguins and swans whilst a further pattern incorporates lobsters. One of the most striking Urbato designs is for a moon flask which depicts a cockerel set against a blazing sun on one side and an owl with a half moon in the background on the reverse.

The decorations were applied to a wide range of articles including vases, jugs, powder bowls, plaques and jardinieres. In addition, the pattern books record designs for inkpots, tea caddies, candlesticks and clock cases.

Spano Lustra

The Spano Lustra range also comprised primarily sgraffito decorations but in one or two colours only. However, as the name suggests, the wares were completed by a covering of iridescent lustres which were applied in a liquid state or obtained by fumes in the kiln according to the tint required. Flowers and leaves are the basis of many of the designs, repeating patterns being a popular device.

The range also included wares, lustred over plain or shaded pale colours, particlularly in the Dainty and Shell shapes of toilet sets.

Pastello

The Pastello decorations consisted of figures, flowers and various natural objects executed on a dark ground, cameo fashion, in a semi-transparent paste. An article in the Artist periodical of 1899 stated : *'The figures show an advance on anything of the kind previously produced in the excellence of design, correctness of drawing, and delicacy of modelling'*.

Few examples appear to have survived although one pattern features a cottage with a smoking chimney, the smoke spiralling sinuously upwards, all set against a predominantly yellow background.

Primitif

Unfortunately, very little is known about this range although it appears to have been based upon 'random' glaze effects. The same article in the Artist reported that : *'In this the effects are obtained (as is the case in the finest antique Japanese and Chinese pottery) by what may be described as 'directed accident'. The effects are all accidental, but are always more or less under the control of the artist, who knows with tolerable accuracy what the general effect will be, but who never knows exactly what delightful passages of colour may gather in certain parts or what beautiful play of textures and lines, like the swirl of water round and over stepping stones in a brook. It requires an artist too to know what to add and what to leave alone."*

Urbato and Spano-Lustra earthenwares with Fola lamps to front

A selection of Intarsio clocks and character tea and coffee pots

Intarsio animal, fish and bird subjects

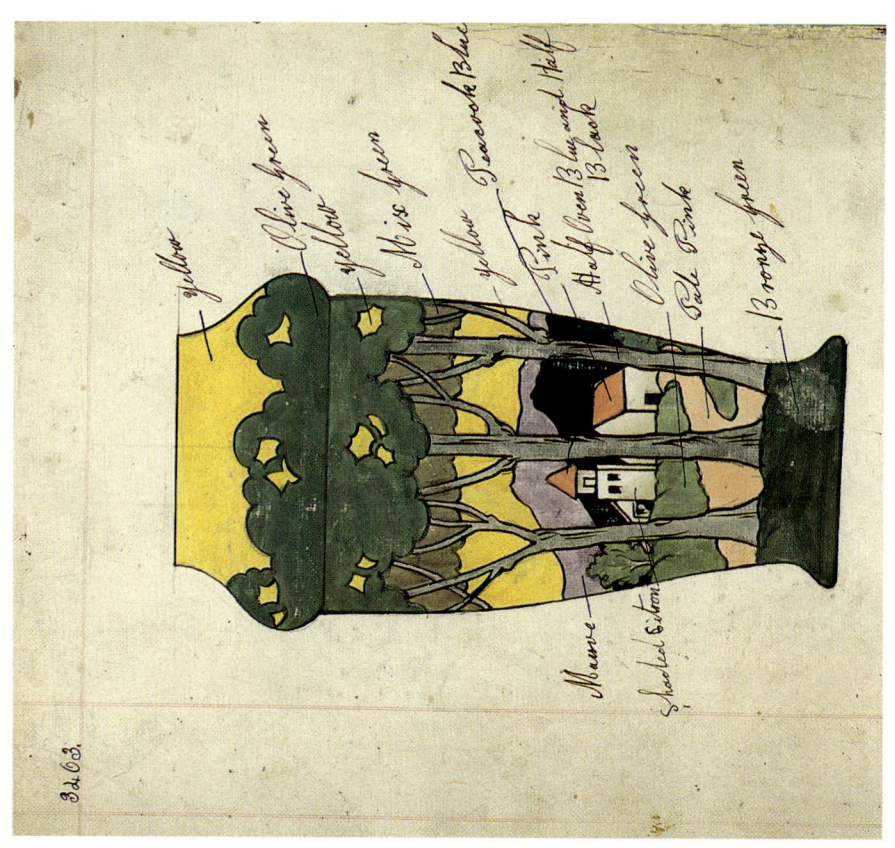

Pages from the pattern book

Examples of Intarsio designs including an advertising plaque

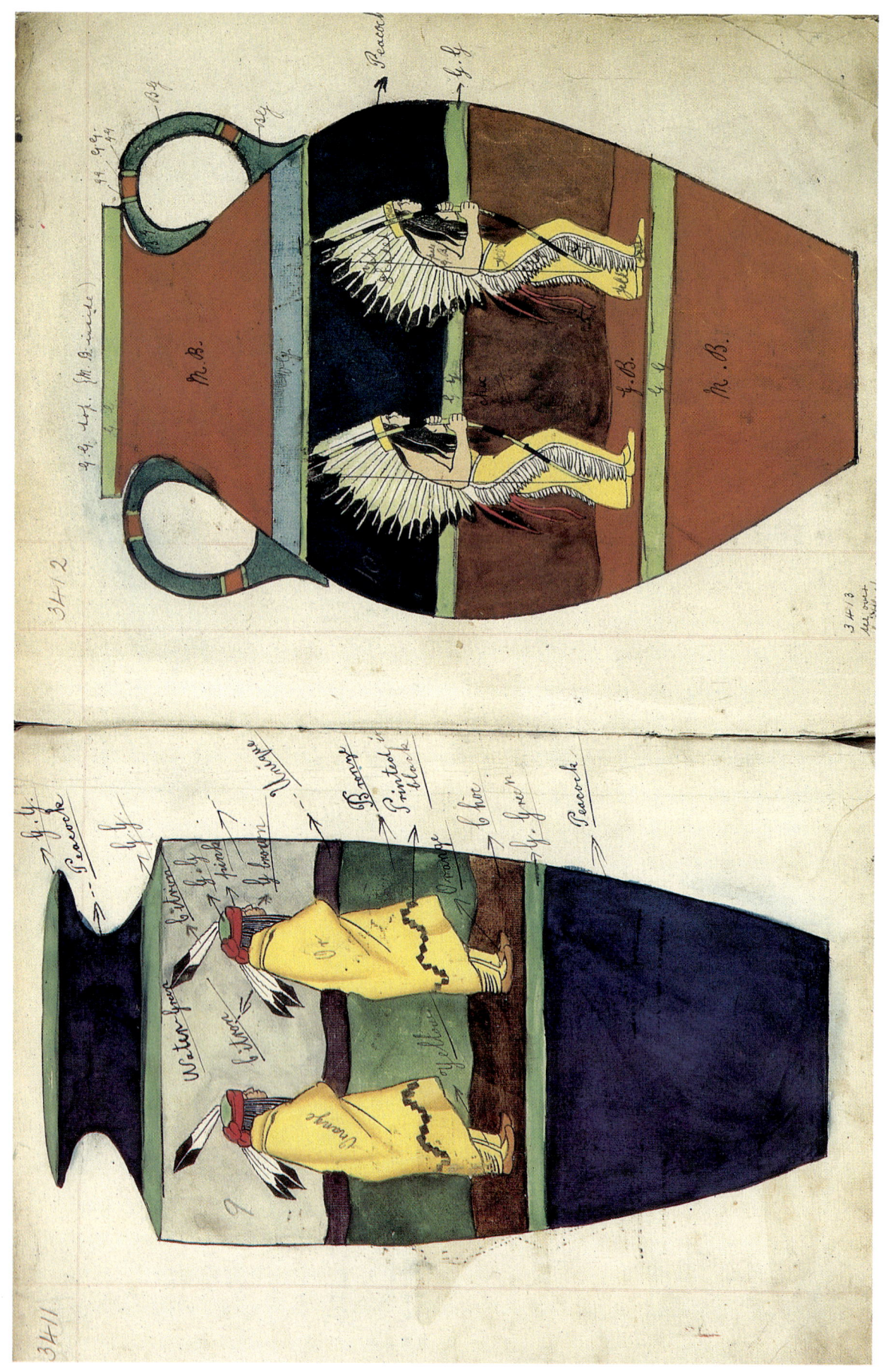

Illustrations from the pattern book, probably for Intarsio designs

72

Various Intarsio patterns including Shakespeare subjects and a Monk character jug

Intarsio stick stand

Umbrella stand for promotional use by shops

3183	Imperial Teapot. Representation of a crown; pink background with orange highlights, finished in blue.
3195	Flowerpots (5 Sizes). Large flowers in red, purple and bronze green with green leaves; blue rim.
3246	Kruger Teapot. Green jacket with blue collar, vest white with orange buttons, brown trousers, face and hands flesh colour, pink warts (!).
3253	Round Footed Fern Box. Green buttercups, shaded in blue, with green leaves on a bronze green background.
3262	Tobacco Jar. Ducklings, shaded yellow and orange, on a green background.
3279	Vase. Farmyard design featuring a procession of cockerels, geese, chicks and hens moving from left to right; decorated in colours; yellow buttercups to top; blue background.
3280	Lidded Vase/Jar. Panel of turkeys, decorated in colours; abstract pattern above and below.
3281	Vase. Farmyard design featuring a procession of hens, cockerels and chicks moving from right to left with a fence in the background; decorated in colours.
3282	Tobacco Jar. Three elderly men in period dress seated, drinking and smoking long-stemmed pipes, creating clouds of smoke; a black cat sits with them; decorated in colours.
3283	Vase. Two panels of swimming fish - large panel around body, small around the neck; decorated in colours.
3307	Biscuit Jar. Large irises in purple and mauve with yellow centres, orange and brown leaves against a green background.
3311	Cat. Blue and yellow background with Fleur de Lys design.
3312	Cat. Yellow background with green leaves all over.
3313	Cat. Green background with ten rats scattered over.
3321	Small Cat. As 3311.
3322	Small Cat. As 3313.
3324	Small Cat. Farmyard Scene.
3329	Clock. Man in period dress, carrying a lamp, walking the streets; text of "Wake Up And Get To Business"; decorated in colours.
3330	Clock. Cavalier style gentleman on left-hand side doffing his cap and bowing deeply to girl on right-hand side who is about to curtsey in acknowledgement. Sunflower in a pot in central panel between. Decorated in colours. Text of "The Time O Day".
3331	Clock. Man in country dress blowing a horn and beating a cymbal in front of a brick wall with trees beyond; text of "Keep Time"; decorated in colours.
3333	Vase. Panel of lambs skipping across grass in front of the base of several trees; decorated in colours; small pink flowers in panels at shoulder and base.

3334	Vase. Large flowers shaded in pink, red and brown on a green background; leaves below on orange background.
3335	Vase. Large blue flowers with green centres with flowing brown and pearl stems and leaveson a yellow background.
3336	Vase. Head and shoulders of a woman, having long brown hair, standing on a wooden balcony looking out; plants in containers on the ledge in front of her; tulip below the balcony and trees above; decorated in colours.
3338	Small cat. Decorated as 3312.
3339	Vase. Witch on a broomstick dressed in a mauve dress and brown cloak; blue sky with yellow half-moon, green ground; text of "Ill Luck Fly Away" around the shoulder.
3340	Vase. Rampant red lions in panel round neck; herald blowing a horn, dressed in a tunic decorated with lions in quartered panels; stylised green foliage; brown background.
3343	Vase. Ladies in medieval dress crossing a brick built bridge; irises in the water beneath; decorated in colours.
3351	Three-Handled Mug (Large size). Large pink flowers with blue centres and green leaves on a green background; brown finish.
3352	Vase. Sinuous brown tree with pink fruit on green foliage growing from green grass into the blue sky.
3353	Vase. River flowing under brick-built bridge with fruit tree.
3354	Vase. Sinuous brown tree with pink fruit and foliage in greens, growing from green grass; blue background.
3356	Face of Chamberlain.
3357	Face of Lord Salisbury
3358	Face of Sir W Harcourt.
3359	Face of Lord Balfour.
3360	Face of Lord Rosebery.
3361	Face of Sir H Campbell Bannerman.
3372	Coffee Pot. Chamberlain.
3373	Coffee Pot. Lord Salisbury
3374	Coffee Pot. Lord Rosebery.
3379	Vase. Kingfisher standing on tree branch; decorated in colours; brown background.
3380	Vase. Fruit trees with geese walking between them on green grass; blue sky with fluffy white clouds.
3381	Vase. Deep border rim of jester's heads dressed in pink hoods against a yellow background; blue for main body of vase; thin border of ringing bells in yellow on a brown background near base.

3382	Vase. Dutch boy dressed in a blue tunic, brown trousers and clogs standing in front of a pool with the base of a windmill behind; Dutch girl dressed in a pink hat, clogs and apron carrying a basket with fields and trees behind.
3383	Jug. Central roundel featuring a quartered Royal Crest of lions and harps with English rose to either side.
3384	Vase. Full figures of King and Queen in full ceremonial robes; King holding orb and sceptre; Queen holding sceptre.(NB Probably Coronation robes which would indicate a date of circa 1901/2.)
3385	Vase. Top border as 3048; front decorated with the King as 3384; back decorated with armorial bearing as 3383.
3386	Vase. As 3385 but Queen replacing King.
3387	Vase. Large irises in purple and mauve with leaves in greens on a brown background.
3388	Three-Legged Bowl/Tazza. Deep panel of swimming fish against a background of blues; finished in brown and green; border of stylised leaves to inside top rim.
3411	Vase. Red Indians standing sideways on having orange blankets with head-dresses of three large feathers, decorated in pink and green; neck and base in blue.
3412	Vase. Red Indians walking carrying bows, dressed in feathered trousers and large feathered head-dresses; neck and base in brown.
3414	Vase. Sprays of small flowers shaded in mauve and pink with intertwining green leaves; background blown in pink.
3426	Rosebowl (Large size). Farmyard scene inside, decorated in colours; floral pattern with leaves outside.
3437	Vase. Sprays of pink flowers with green intertwining leaves on a green background; border of overlapping scales pattern in pink and green to neck.
3455	Clock. Young man and woman in medieval dress holding hands across a sundial; trees framing clock hole with bird flying above; decorated in colours; text of "The Days May Come The Days May Go" across the bottom; finished in brown.
3457	Jug. Rotund man holding a large tankard, sitting back in a wooden chair; woman bending forward with a covered jug; young man to the other side with jugs; wooden table with bread on plate; period dress. Reverse panel of rotund man slumped asleep in the chair and three empty jugs on the floor. Text of "What An Intolerable Deal Of Sack To Such A Pitiful Proprtion Of Bread".Decorated in colours.
3458	Tobacco Jar (?). Man's head with wire-rimmed glasses, smoking a pipe and enveloped by clouds of smoke; brown background, finished in green.
3459	Scotchman. No detail.
3460	Irishman. No detail.
3461	Vase. Sailing galleon centred against clouds; large pink flowers and buds at neck.

3463	Vase. Red-roofed church (or house) behind trees to foreground; path leading from trees to house; decorated in colours.
3464	Vase. Turretted castle with red roofs and yellow walls having green trees and bushes clustered around its base, one stylised tree to the foreground; bird motif to neck.
3465	Vase. Shakespeare subjects. One panel of Malvolio and one panel of Sir Toby Belch.
3466	Vase/Flask. Shakespeare subjects. One side having a figure of Macbeth with sword drawn and holding a shield and the caption "Macbeth Act V Scene VII; the other side features a turretted castle. Text of "Of All Men Else I Have Avoided Thee Glamis" around the neck.
3467	Vase. Shakespeare subjects. One side having a figure of Hamlet and the caption "Hamlet Act V Scene I"; the other side showing a castle set on rocks. Text of "Dost Know This Water" around the neck.
3468	Vase. Shakespeare subjects. One side showing a scene of two night watchmen challenging two others and the caption "Much Ado About Nothing Act III Scene III; reverse side shows same four figures conversing. Text of "We Charge You In The Prince's Name, Stand".
3469	Vase. Large tree to the foreground with watermill, bridge and house behind; fluffy white clouds in a blue sky above; base finished around in blue to represent river; decorated in colours.
3470	Shakespeare subjects. Ariel on one side with the text "Tempest Act V Scene I"; reverse side showing Puck and the text "Midsummer Nights Dream Act II Scene I".
3471	Yorick. Jester sitting at a table talking to model jester's head on stick in jug. (Drawing only).
7033	Teapot. Two panels of figures in period dress; lady to the right offering teapot to man on the left who is holding out a teacup. Printed sunflowers between the two panels in green, orange and red.
7039	Vesper Jug. Panels of monks, decorated in colours, finished in gold; text of "A Chirping Cup is My Matin Song And The Vesper Bell is My Bowl Ding Dong".
7240	Tobacco Jar. Irishman, John Bull and Scotchman standing arms linked; decorated in colours.
7240A	Tobacco Jar. Frockcoated old gentleman sitting, holding a long-stemmed pipe and raising his glass.
7331	Pelican Pot (5 Sizes : 4" - 8"). Delphic Dawn, featuring windmill and buildings with water to foreground; printed in brown, blown in ivory, enamalled and blown again in brown.
7332	Pelican Pots (5 Sizes : 4" - 8"). Delphic Sunset, featuring a windmill with landing stage, small sailing boats on the water around; printed in brown, blown in greens, deep red sky.

7336	Plain Pots, Vases, Small Vases, China Vases. Delphic Green, featuring sailing boats in browns, background blown in greens.
7339	Plain Pot. Honesty; printed in green; groundlayed in pink and green, shaded; floral jungle print all over as background; Honesty tinted; pearl lustre all over.
7371	Vases, Kings Toilet etc. Hunting Subjects; printed in brown and enamalled in colours; edged in green.
7372	Motoring Subjects; four scenes, printed in black and enamalled in colours; finished in gold.

7373	Peter Pan. Three scenes, printed in brown and enamalled in colours, finished in green, as follows :
	1. Captain Hook sitting on the quayside with his ship behind him and the text :
	    Yo Ho, Yo Ho, The Pirate Life!
	    The flag o'skull and bones
	    A merry hour - a hempen rope!
	    And Hey for Davey Jones
	
	2. The three children having a pillow fight in the cave nursery with the text :
	    High Jinks in the Cave Nursery
	    A bolster and a pillow dance
	
	3. Bedroom scene with Nana and Peter Pan with the text :
	    Nana, the faithful nurse
	    Is surprised by Peter

7374	Dickens Subjects. Two scenes, printed in brown and enamalled in colours, finished in gold, as follows :
	1. The Artful Dodger meeting Oliver at the roadside with the text :
	    Hullo My Covey, What's The Row?
	
	2. Mr Pickwick slumped in a wheelbarrow with three companions with the text :
	    Who Are You, You Rascal. What's Your Name?

7375	Golf Subjects. Two scenes, printed in brown and enamalled in colours.
7376	Fathers Of Empire being an Irishman, John Bull and a Scotsman as 7240. (Rd 407992). For china see 10238.
7377	Screaming devils in green with mauve wings, finished in gold.
7378	Smoker. Seated gentleman dressed in a red jacket, brown breeches and a green hat smoking a long-stemmed pipe creating clouds of smoke, jug (of ale?) at his side on the floor.
7416	Vases. Thunderstorm. Fishing boats printed in black, sails and mountains pencilled in pink, shaded in pink and blue fused to purples.
7424	May Toilet. Cottage with smoking chimney amongst trees, the smoke streaming up into the sky; yellow background. (This pattern has been seen with the Pastello series name).

7425   Vase. Noonday; yachting scenes with boats in brown and background blown in colours; gold finish.

7426   Vase. Tristo Ware; large iris in red with red and blue leaves against a gold background; blue neck.

7430   American Shape Jug. River scene with monks returning from fishing with a small catch; dogs running around including one running over the bridge with a fish in its mouth, chased by an irate monk. Decorated in colours.

7431   Cambridge Jugs. Merry Wives Of Windsor, two scenes; decorated in colours with the text :
> I see you are obsequious
> In Your Love
> I love thee, and none but thee,
> Let me creep in here.

7432   Jugs. Three monks fishing by the river, one with a rod, one with a net and one watching; decorated in colours with the text :
> Tomorrow will be Friday
> Every brother his rod he took
> Every rod had a line and a hook
> Every hook had a bait so fine
> And thus they sang in the Evenshine
> Tomorrow will be Friday.

A further unnamed pattern book details patterns in the range 10.001 to 12.091, although many of the numbers were not used. The designs are primarily for ornamental articles and include a series of Scottish Motto Wares.

Of particular interest is a sequence of patterns designated for pairs of wall plaques, detailed below.

11.043	14" Plaque	Hare and Magpies
11.044	14" Plaque	Birds and Grasses
11.045	14" Plaque	Brittany Heads
11.046	14" Plaque	Fish and Lobster
11.047	12" Plaque	Landscape Views
11.048	8: Plaque	Birds
11.049	12: Plaque	Sea Views
11.050	10} Plaque	Dutch Characters
11.051	10" Plaque	Castles
11.052	12" Plaque	Peacocks
11.053	8" Plaque	Fish and Lobster
11.054	10" Plaque	Queen and Knave of Hearts

Intarsio patterns showing the Art Nouveau influence

Examples of Intarsio featuring floral motifs

A selection of Intarsio, further illustrating the variety of shapes employed

Intarsio wares together with a Cloisello vase (front left)

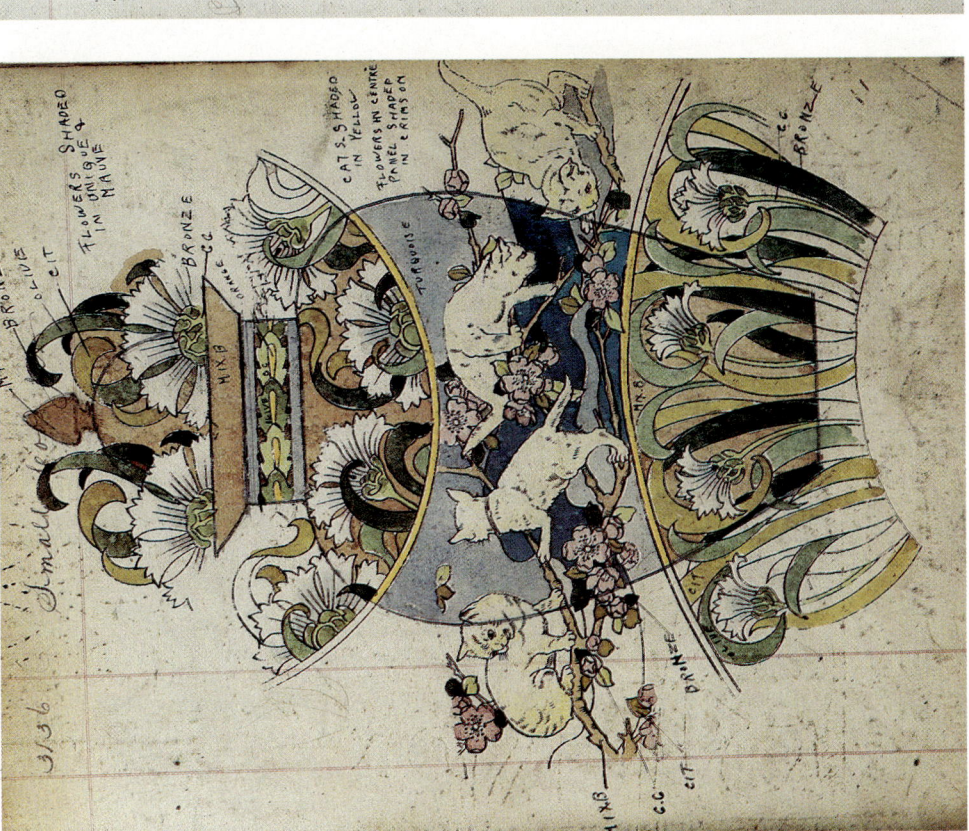

Extracts from the pattern book

Examples of Faience showing the range of different styles and decorating techniques used; of particular interest is the Grotesque jug (centre). The jug and vase (centre and front left) are a Pastello design.

Highly decorated earthenwares, some of which carry a Faience backstamp and/or the pattern name Old Chelsea

Page from the pattern book

Appendix A : Bibliography

Ceramic Art Of Great Britain
Llewellyn Jewitt

People Of The Potteries, A Dictionary of Local Biography
Edited by Denis Stuart; Department of Adult Education, University of Keele

Shelley Potteries, The History and Production of a Staffordshire Family of Potters
Watkins, Harvey & Senft; Barrie & Jenkins

Rhead Artists & Potters 1870 - 1950
Bernard Bumpus; Exhibition Catalogue 1986/87

Historic Building Survey Of Foley Potteries
City of Stoke-on-Trent, 1983

A History Of Fenton
Young & Jenkins

Encyclopedia Of Pottery & Porcelain, 19th and 20th Centuries
Elizabeth Cameron; Faber & Faber

Encyclopedia Of British Art Pottery 1870 - 1920
Victoria Bergesen; Barrie & Jenkins

The Artist, 1899

Pottery Gazette & Glass Trade Review

Appendix B : Backstamps

The following backstamps provide a useful guide to dating.

James Wileman
Examples of backstamps used 1870 - 1892

Wileman & Co

1872 - 1890
Used on all wares
Variations include:
– 'ENGLAND' added
– 'Made in England' added

1890 - 1910
Used on all wares
Variations include :
– range names were incorporated for some earthenwares, such as 'Urbato', 'Spano-Lustra' and 'Faience'.
– The words 'The Foley China' replaced 'The Foley'.

90

Shelley

1910 – 1925
Used on all wares

Variations include :
- the words 'Late Foley' were incorporated between 1910 and 1916;
- pattern names were incorporated for some earthenwares, such as 'Cloisello' and 'Flamboyant';
- some lustre wares carry a facsimile 'Walter Slater' signature.

1910 – 1945
Used on heraldic miniatures.

1925 – 1945
Used on all wares

Variations include :
- the words 'Fine Bone China' were added from 1945;
- some pattern names were incorporated for both china and earthenwares, such as 'Chelsea', 'Versaille', 'Melody' and 'Maytime'.

1930 – 1932
Used only on china

NB. This mark is also found on miniatures produced in the 1950's.

1936 – 1937
Used on commemoratives only.

Appendix C : Registered Numbers

The following registered numbers allocated to Wileman during the years 1884 to 1900 have been extracted from the Official Journal of Patents which is available at the Public Records Office.

Year	Numbers	Year	Numbers	Year	Numbers
1884	3931	**1891**	164130	**1901**	368024
	6559		164516		370315
	11446		173373		372764
1885	34339		175636		379151 – 3
	34404		175836		380373 – 5
	36808		181135		380408
	40405	**1892**	196305 – 8		380581
1886	49676		198245		380708
	57380		199684	**1902**	384295
	60650	**1893**	206622		388120
	60868		208329		391255
1887	64761		208365		397890 – 3
	65169		212502		398711
	68702		212544	**1903**	402479
	73363		213327		404405
	74706	**1894**	233180		407992
	79256	**1896**	270002		408695
	84175		272101		412401
	88523		272764		412402
1888	91357 – 8		276278 – 9		412403 – 10
	91681		276548		416320
	92158		276842 – 7		417630
	94675		283662	**1904**	424619
	97379		283973		425155 – 7
	99001	**1897**	290929		430123
	103613		306302		430208
	106682		308538		430326
	114176	**1898**	318081		430994
	115510		330274 – 309		435556
1889	117220		330395		435558
	118299 – 301		330702	**1905**	447136 – 42
	119503 – 5		330911 – 12		447226 – 31
	119507	**1899**	331253		447312
	124057		331867 – 9		448983
	131562		331956 – 9		452342
	133642		333035		453983
	134987		333452		456392
1890	145096		334904 – 6		468736
	145220		336411 – 2		470748
	145819		337244	**1906**	471479
	146299		337994 – 9		472025
	150035	**1900**	351373		472950
	151830		354780		481087
	153594		356481	**1907**	496830
	157683		360460		497610
	157867		364131	**1910**	553854
	160558		364152 – 3		554407
	160768		364386		558497
			365797		

Appendix D : China Reference Guide

The earliest remaining pattern book begins in 1882 with number 3348, although it does provide evidence of earlier pattern numbers.

Around 1890, a new series of pattern numbers began at 6002 and ran concurrently with the earlier series which ceased at 6001, when an overlap became apparent, and continued at 9002.

An annotation against number 10553, dated January 25th 1911, indicates that both series were amalgamated at that point, continuing from 8313 (the number reached in the second series at the time) until number 9001, in 1913. As this then overlapped with the first series, the pattern numbers continued from 10554. This is illustrated below.

Book	Numbers	Date
1	3348 – 4970	1882 – 1893
2	4971 – 6001	1893 – 1897
	9002 – 9269	1897 – 1901
3	9270 – 10548	1901 – 1910
4	6002 – 6843	1890 – 1895
5	6844 – 7307	1895 – 1901
6	7308 – 7899	1901 – 1906
7	7900 – 8312	1906 – Jan 1911
	8313 – 8810	Jan 1911 – 1913
8	10549 – 10553	Jan 1911 – Jan 1911
	8811 – 9001	1913 – 1913
	10554 – 11140	1913 – 1919
9	New Book	April 1919
	transfer of earlier numbers still in use then	
	11141 – 11712	1919 – 1929

The following pages list the china pattern numbers that fall within the period 1882 to 1910 together with the shape range(s) to which they were applied. Brief pattern descriptions are also given in some instances. Those entries with identical pattern names indicate colour variations of the same design.

The information has been compiled from the original pattern books, some of which are in poor condition. Hence, some entries are unfortunately incomplete.

August 1882

3348		Ivy Pattern; rustic cup handle	Victoria	Rose Wreaths & Forget-me-nots
3349 to 3365		Japonica & Bird	-	Thistle
3366 to 3369		Blackberry	-	Sprig & Leaf
3370		Japonica	-	Japan - blue & red
3371		Blackberry	-	Wild Rose
3372		Japonica	-	Apple Blossom
3373		Japonica; rustic cup handle	-	Blackthorn
3374		Blackberry	-	Blackberry
3375		Dog Rose	-	Children in country scene
3376		Blackberry	-	Japonica - enamelled
3377 to 3379		As 3323	-	Birds - enamelled
3380		Printed Wreaths	-	Not used
3381		Floral Border	-	As 3291
3382 to 3383		Japonica & Bird	-	As 2209
3384		Bird	-	As 3229
3385		Rose	-	As 2694
3386		Not used	-	Not used
3387 to 3390		As 3324	-	As 2065
3391		Blackberry	-	As 3167
3392		Verbena	-	As 2572
3393		Hawthorn & Passion Flower	Worcester, Minton	As 2720
3394		Not used	Victoria	Birds
3395		Apple Blossom	-	Wild Roses & Butterfly
3396		Blackthorn Blossom	Worcester	Border Pattern
3397		Sprigs & Berries	-	Wild Roses & Butterfly
3398		Sunflower	-	As 3176
3399 to 3407		Small Floral Borders	-	As 3271
3408		As 3297	-	As 3185
3409		Moss Rose	-	As 3159
3410		Japonica & Bird	-	As 3158
3411		Sunflower	-	As 3293
3412	Victoria	Floral Border	-	As 3276
3413		Wild Rose	Victoria	E Smith's Ivy
3414		Fine black line	Victoria	Japan (Rd No 3931)
3415		Fine red line	Victoria	As 3180
3416		Plain red edge	-	As 3179
3417 to 3419	Worcester, Minton	Printed Palm	-	Border Patterns
3420		Rose Wreaths & Forget-me-nots	-	Wild Roses & Butterfly
3421				As 3083
3422				Blackthorn
3423				
3424 to 3425				
3426 to 3427				
3428 to 3429				
3430 to 3431				
3432				
3433				
3434				
3435				
3436				
3437				
3438				
3439				
3440				
3441				
3442				
3443				
3444				
3445				
3446 to 3447				
3448				
3449 to 3453				
3454				
3455				
3456				
3457				
3458				
3459				
3460				
3461				
3462 to 3463				
3464				
3465				
3466				
3467 to 3470				
3471 to 3473				
3474				
3475				

No.	Shape	Pattern
3476	Square (QA)	Japan
3477 to 3478	Victoria	Ivy, as 3462
3479	Victoria	Ivy, as 3281
3480	Victoria	As 3083
3481	Victoria	Ivy
3482	Victoria	Wild Roses & Butterfly
3483 to 3487	Victoria	Gothic Border (Rd No 11446)
3488	Square QA, Daisy	Ivy
3489	Square QA	Wild Roses & Butterfly
3490	Square QA	Blackberry
3491 to 3493	Square QA	Wild Roses & Butterfly
3494 to 3495	Square QA	Ivy
3496 to 3497	Square Qa	Blackberry
3498	Square QA	Thistle Border
3499	Square QA, Victoria	Ivy
3500 to 3503	Victoria	Clematis
3504 to 3507	Square QA	Clematis
3508	Victoria	Border Print
3509	Square QA	Maroon, cross hatched panels
3510	Victoria	Gothis Border, as 3483
3511 to 3514	Square QA	Printed Season Views
3515 to 3522	Victoria	Border Prints
3523 to 3526	-	Cancelled
3527	Victoria	Japonica Flowers
3528	Victoria	Border Design
3529 to 3531	Square QA	Orchids
3532	Square QA, Victoria, Worcester	Japan - oriental Flowers
3533	Victoria	Blue line border
3534	Victoria, Minton	Blackberries
3535	Victoria, Minton	Wild Roses & Butterfly
3536 to 3537	Victoria, Minton	Apple Blossom
3538	Victoria, Minton	Blackberry
3539	Victoria, Minton	Wild Roses & Butterfly
3540	Victoria, Minton	Japonica Flowers
3541	Victoria, Minton	Printed Seasons Views
3542	Square QA	Ivy
3543	Square QA, Victoria	Japan (black) - Oriental Rose
3544 to 3547	Square QA, Victoria, Worcester	Thistle
3548	Victoria	Gothic Border, as 3483
3549 to 3553	Square QA, Victoria	Roses
3554	Victoria	Japan - black & red oriental flowers
3555	Victoria	Japan - blue & red oriental flowers
3556	Square QA	Wild Rose
3557	-	Not used
3558	Victoria	Thistle
3559	Square QA	Apple Blossom
3560	Victoria	Japan - Flowers & Tree (Rd 36808)
3561	Square QA	As 3560
3562	Victoria	As 3560
3563	Square QA	As 3560

February 1886

No.	Shape	Pattern
3564	Worcester	Badge
3565 to 3566	Minton Coffee	Badge
3567	Square QA	Turquoise & gold
3568 to 3575	Square QA	Blackberries
3576 to 3578	Square QA, Victoria	Not used
3579 to 3580	-	Thistle Border
3581	Victoria	Floral Border
3582	Victoria, Minton	Badge
3583	Gladstone	Badge
3584	Worcester	Badge
3585	Minton	Badge
3586 to 3587	Worcester	Sprigs
3588	Victoria	Thistle
3589	Victoria	Bands
3590 to 3592	Victoria	As 1992
3593	Victoria, Square QA	Bands
3594 to 3596	Victoria	Badge
3597	Victoria	Roses, as 3549
3598 to 3599	Victoria	

May 1886

No.	Shape	Pattern
3600	Victoria	Badge
3601	Roman Breakfast	Badge

September 1886

3602	Roman	Badge
3603	Minton	Badge
3604 to 3605	Victoria, Worcester	Bramble
3606	-	Not used
3607	Victoria, Worcester	Bramble
3608	Square QA	Thistle, as 3581
3609	Square QA	As 3480
3610 to 3613	Square QA	Clover
3614 to 3616	Square QA	Scenery
3617	Square QA	Scenery - enamalled
3618	Roman	Badge
3619	Square QA	Wild Roses & Butterfly
3620	Square QA	As 3229
3621	Square QA	Clover
3622	Victoria, Square	As 3313
3623 to 3624	Victoria, Square	Roses, as 3549
3625 to 3628	Victoria	Clover

December 1886

3629 to 3631	Minton	Badge
3632	Jubilee Flute	Japan - black border
3633	Jubilee Flute	Japan - Oriental Flowers, as 3532
3634 to 3636	Jubilee Flute	Thistle
3637 to 3639	Jubilee Flute	Clover
3640	Jubilee Flute	Wild Roses & Butterfly
3641	Jubilee Flute	Clover - enamalled

January 1887

3642 to 3643	Turkish Cans	Japan, as 3464; special order
3644	Square QA	Japan - black border, as 3632
3645 to 3647	Jubilee Flute	Bramble
3648 to 3650	Jubilee Flute	Shamrock
3651	Jubilee Flute	Clover
3652	Roman	Badge
3653 to 3654	Minton	Badge
3655	Victoria	Badge

3656 to 3658	Victoria	Thistle
3659 to 3660	Albert	Shamrock
3661	Albert	Bramble
3662	Roman	Badge
3663	Victoria	Bramble
3664	Victoria	Shamrock
3665 to 3667	Square QA	Shamrock
3668	Roman	Badge
3669 to 3671	Victoria	Shamrock
3672	Albert	Shamrock
3673	Victoria	As 3176
3674	Minton	As 3302
3675	Albert	Japan - Black
3676 to 3678	Square QA	Bramble
3679 to 3681	Square QA	Clover
3682 to 3684	Square QA	Shamrock
3685	Albert	Shamrock
3686	Gladstone	Badge
3687	Victoria	Badge
3688	Roman	Badge
3689	Gladstone	Badge
3690	Albert	Japan - Blue
3691	Albert	Wild Roses & Butterfly
3692	Victoria	Japan, as 3464; burnished gold
3693	Minton	Badge
3694	Albert	Clover

August 1887

3695 to 3697	Square Fluted	Shamrock
3698 to 3700	Square Fluted	Thistle
3701 to 3703	Square Fluted	Bramble
3704 to 3706	Square Fluted	Clover
3707	Alex, Square QA	Clover - enamalled (Rd 57380)
3708	Alex, Square QA	Wild Roses & Butterfly
3709 to 3710	Alex, Square QA	Roses
3711 to 3721	Victoria	Floral Sprigs
3722	Alex	Cornflower
3723	Alex, Square QA	Cornflower
3724	Alex	Cornflower

97

3725	Alex	Japan - Red & black (RD 84175)	3790	-	Not used
3726	Minton Breakfast	Badge	3791 to 3794	Victoria	Sprigs
3727	Albert	Shamrock	3795	Victoria	Jasmine - enamelled
3728 to 3729	Alex	Floral	3796	Victoria, Worcester	Dolley Varden print
3730	Alex, Square QA, Daisy, Lily	Japan - Black	3797 to 3801	Victoria, Worcester	Oak Border
3731	Paris	Badge	3802 to 3805	Victoria	Bramble
3732	Victoria	Badge	3806 to 3809	Victoria	Thistle
3733	Minton Breakfast	Badge	3810 to 3813	Victoria	Shamrock
3734	Victoria Breakfast	Badge	3814 to 3817	Victoria	Seasons
3735	Minton Breakfast	Badge	3818 to 3821	Lily	Daisy & Butterfly
3736	Victoria Irish	Badge	3822 to 3832	-	Not used
3737	Alex	Japan - Blue & red (Rd 88523)	3833	Victoria, Worcester	Oak Border
3738 to 3740	Alex	Clover	3834	Alex	Japanese Rose
3741	Victoria	As 3593	3835	Lily	Japanese Rose
3742	Victoria	Badge	3836	Alex	Japanese Rose
3743	Paris	As 1732	3837	Lily	Japanese Rose
3744 to 3749	Alex	Dolley Varden print (Rd 92158)	3838	Alex	Japanese Rose
3750	Alex, Worcester	Dolley Varden print (Rd 92158)	3839	Lily	Japanese Rose
3751 to 3752	Victoria	Badge	3840	Alex	Japanese Rose
3753 to 3757	Alex	Honeysuckle	3841	Lily	Japanese Rose
3758	Alex	Honeysuckle - enamalled	3842	Alex	Gold & Silver Thorns
3759	Square QA	Honeysuckle - enamalled	3843	Lily	Gold & Silver Thorns
3760 to 3761	Square QA	Honeysuckle	3844	Alex	Gold & Silver Thorns
3762 to 3763	-	Not used	3845	Lily	Gold & Silver Thorns
3764	Square QA	Honeysuckle - enamalled	3846	Alex	Gold & Silver Thorns
3765	Alex	Clover	3847	Lily	Gold & Silver Thorns
3766	Alex, Square QA	Japan - Honeysuckle, red & black	3848	Alex	Gold & Silver Thorns
3767 to 3770	Albert	Honeysuckle	3849	Lily	Gold & Silver Thorns
3771	Albert	Honeysuckle - enamalled	3850	Alex	Gold & Silver Thorns
3772 to 3773	-	Not used	3851	Lily	Gold & Silver Thorns
3774	Square QA	As 3593, all gold	3852	Lily	Japan - black & red (Rd 119507)
3775	Worcester	Japan, as 3725 (Rd 84175)	3853 to 3855	Worcester	Gold Border
3776	Victoria Breakfast	Badge	3856	Victoria	As 3480
3777	Worcester Breakfast	Badge	3857	Victoria	As 3713
3778 to 3781	Albert	Cornflower	3858	Minton	Blue & pink edge
3782 to 3786	Victoria	Honeysuckle	3859	Minton	Bands
3787	-	Not used	3860	Worcester	Shamrock
3788	Minton	Floral Sprig	3861 to 3867	Lily	Panelled Prints
3789	Alex	Cornflower	3868	Lily	As 3847
			3869	Worcester	As 3853

98

3870 to 3878	Lily	Margarette Print (Rd 124057)		3931	Lily	Japan - Oriental Flowers, red
3879 to 3883	Victoria	Oak Border		3932 to 3938	Lily	Ornament Festooned
3884	-	Not used		3939	Worcester	Badge
3885	Lily	Panelled Prints		3940	Minton	Badge
3886 to 3887	Alex	Gold & Silver Thorns		3941	Gladstone	Badge
3888 to 3896	Victoria	Narrow Printed Border		3942	Alex	Japan, as 3725 (Rd 84175)
3897	Worcester	Gold Border		3943	Worcester	Badge
3898	Minton Breakfast	Badge		3944 to 3949	Alex	Wild Rose
3899	Egg	Special shape for JMcDs		3950	Worcester	Wild Rose
3900	Silver	Badge		3951 to 3952	Alex	Wild Rose
3901	Gladstone	Badge		3953	Lily	Chrysanthemum Sprigs
3902	Roman	Badge		3954 to 3955	-	Not used
3903	Minton Breakfast	Badge		3956 to 3959	Lily	Chrysanthemum Sprigs
3904	Hammersley Can	Badge		3960 to 3965	-	Not used
				3966	Daisy	Japan - red & black
July 1889				3967	Lily	Ornament, as 3934
				3968 to 3970	Alex	Sprigs
3905	Worcester Breakfast	Badge		3971	Lily	Japan, as 3852
3906	Gladstone Breakfast	Badge		3972	Minton Coffee Can	Badge
3907	Lily	Daisy Wreath - black & red		3973	Lily	Chrysanthemum Sprays
3908	Victoria	Badge		3974	Lily	Flowers & Butterflies
3909	Gladstone	Badge		3975	Albert	Flowers & Butterflies
3910	Hammersley Dundee	Badge		3976	-	Not used
				3977	Minton Irish	Badge
August 1889				3978	Worcester	Badge
				3979		Not used
3911	Egg Cups	Badge		3980	Victoria	Aster Sprays
3912	Fruit Tray	As 6031		3981	Alex	Aster Sprays
3913	Fruit Tray	Daisy Border		3982	Lily	Aster Sprays
3914	Victoria	Floral Sprigs		3983	Worcester	Aster Sprays
3915	Alex	Buttercups - enamalled		3984	Minton Breakfast	Aster Sprays
3916 to 3922	-	Not used		3985	Daisy	Aster Sprays
3923	Worcester	Panelled Prints		3986 to 3988	-	Not used
3924	Worcester	Badge		3989	Alex	Floral Border
3925	Minton	Gold Sprigs		3990 to 3992	Albert Coffee	Jasmine
3926	-	Not used		3993 to 3994	-	Not used
3927	Alex	As 3480		3995	Albert Coffee	Floral Edge
3928	Alex	Floral Sprigs		3996	Alex	Floral Edge
3929	Alex	As 3593		3997 to 4003	Albert Coffee	Jungle Sheet
3930	Alex	Floral Sprigs		4004 to 4005	-	Not used

99

4006	Alex	As 3744 (Rd 92158)	4089	Minton Irish	Badge
4007	Alex	Bramble	4090	Alex	Wild Rose, as 3944
4008	Albert	Bramble	4091 to 4092	Alex	Gold & Silver Thorns, as 3846
4009	Alex	Thistle	4093	Alex	Thistle
4010	Albert	Thistle	4094	Alex	Brambles
4011	Lily	Margarette, as 3870			
4012	Victoria	Oak Border, as 3797	**September 1890**		
4013	Paris Irish	Badge			
4014	Minton Irish	Badge	4095	Roman	Badge
4015	Fruit Dishes	Japan - red print with gold	4096	Alex	Panelled Design
4016	Minton	Badge	4097	Alex	Dresden Flowers
4017	Lily	Chrysanthemum Sprays, as 3953	4098	Lily	Dresden Flowers
4018	Minton	Badge	4099	Paris	Badge
4019 to 4022	Marmalades	Chrysanthemums	4100	Daisy	Gold Thorns
4023	Lily	Japan - red (Rd 146299)	4101 to 4102	Daisy	Gold & Silver Thorns
4024	Alex	Japan - red (Rd 146299)			
4025	Roman	Badge	**October 1890**		
4026 to 4031	Lily, Daisy	Jungle Sheet, special order JMcDs			
4032	Gladstone	Badge	4103	6" Muffins	Badge
4033	Minton Irish	Badge, as 3891	4104 to 4109	Alex	Dresden Flowers
4034	Gladstone Breakfast	Badge	4110 to 4114	-	Not used
4035	Alex	As 3744	4115	Victoria Breakfast	Badge
4036	Victoria	As 3889	4116	Victoria	Spray & Butterfly
4037	Victoria	Border Design, special order	4117	Lily	Spray & Butterfly
4038	Silver Breakfast	Badge	4118	Alex	Spray & Butterfly
4039	Silver	Badge			
4040	Gladstone	Badge	**November 1890**		
4041	Lily	Clover			
4042	Ash Tray (fluted)	Badge	4119	Victoria Breakfast	Badge
4043 to 4058	Alex, Daisy, Dainty, Snowdrop	Plain Colour	**December 1890**		
4059	Victoria	Badge	4120	Minton Irish	Badge
4060	Victoria Breakfast	Badge	4121	-	Not used
4061 to 4070	Victoria	Daisy Border Print	4122	Lily	Thistle (seconds) (Rd 34404)
4071 to 4072	Bute	Daisy Border Print (seconds, NZ)	4123	Daisy, Alex	Bramble (seconds)
4073 to 4074	New York	Daisy Border Print (seconds, NZ)	4124	Daisy, Alex	Clover (seconds)
4075 to 4084	Lily	Daisy Border Print	4125	Daisy, Alex	Thistle (seconds)
4085	-	Not used	4126	Lily	Bramble (seconds)
4086 to 4087	Lily	Daisy Border Print	4127	Lily	Sunflower (seconds)
4088	-	Not used			

100

4128 to 4130	Daisy	Jungle Sheet (seconds)
4131	Fairy	Jungle Sheet (seconds)
4132	Fairy	Clover (seconds)
4133	Fairy	Thistle (seconds)
4134	Fairy	Daisy Border (seconds)
4135	Fairy	Jungle Sheet (seconds)
4136 to 4137	Fairy	Star Pattern (seconds)
4138 to 4139	Lily	Lace Border (seconds)
4140	Daisy	Dresden Flowers (seconds)
4141	Daisy	Jungle Sheet (seconds)
4142	Daisy	Clover (seconds)
4143 to 4144	Lily	Jungle Sheet (seconds)
4145	Lily	Lace Border (seconds)
4146 to 4148	Alex	Jungle Sheet (seconds)
4149	Alex, Daisy	Thistle (seconds)
4150	Lily	Jungle Sheet (seconds)
4151 to 4162	Alex	Basket Of Flowers (Rd 160786)
4163	—	Not used
4164	Alex	Dresden Flowers
4165 to 4167	Victoria	Border Sprays
4168 to 4170	Albert Coffees	Daisy Border
4171 to 4182	Fairy	Star Pattern (Rd 164130)
4183	—	Not used
4184	Shell	Gold with beading
4185	Shell, Empire, Foley	Stippled gold edge
4186	Daisy	Badge
4187 to 4190	—	Not used
4191 to 4202	Lily	Basket Of Flowers
4203 to 4204	—	Not used

March 1891

4205	Minton Irish	Badge
4206	Silver Breakfast	Badge
4207	Victoria Breakfast	Badge

April 1891

4208	Victoria	Badge

May 1891

4209	Silver Breakfast	Badge
4210	Victoria (Milks)	Badge
4211 to 4222	Lily	Dresden Flowers
4223 to 4225	—	Not used
4226 to 4230	Fairy	Border Pattern
4231 to 4242	Fairy	Dresden Flowers
4243	Fairy	Dresden Flowers - enamalled
4244	Fairy	Border Pattern
4245	Victoria	Fern Border
4246	Roman	Badge
4247	Turkish Cans	Japan - Oriental Flowers, red
4248	Turkish Cans	Japan - Oriental Flowers, red & black
4249	Alex	As 3744
4250 to 4252	Fairy	Star Pattern, special order
4253	Fairy	Japan - Oriental Flowers (Rd 145819)
4254	Alex	As 3744
4255	Fairy	Japan - blue & red (Rd 173373)
4256	Gladstone	Bramble
4257	Victoria Breakfast	Badge
4258	Lily	As 3862
4259	Roman Breakfast	Badge
4260	Victoria	Gold Lines & Sprigs
4261	Alex	As 3744
4262	Fairy	Japan - red, as 3852 (Rd 119507)
4263	Lily	Margarette
4264 to 4265	Lily	Daisy Border, special order

July 1891

4266	Gladstone	Badge
4267	Victoria Breakfast	Badge
4268 to 4269	Daisy	As 4228

September 1891

4270	Gladstone	Badge
4271 to 4282	Fairy	Daisy Border

4283 to 4286	-	Not used
4287	Albert Coffee	Daisy Border
4288 to 4291	Daisy	Shell Pattern, special order
4292 to 4297	Victoria	Gothic Border, as 3483
4298 to 4299	-	Not used
4300	Fairy	Convolvulus Print
4301 to 4302	Fairy	Gold Chrystanthemum
4303 to 4306	Fairy	As 6209
4307	Victoria	As 3889
4308 to 4310	Fairy	As 4244
4311 to 4322	Shell	Floral Display
4323 to 4325	-	Not used
4326	Fairy	Japan - black, as 3852 (Rd 119507)

October 1891

4327	Victoria Breakfast	Badge
4328	Stanley Coffee	Ivy Border
4329	Bamboo Coffee	Ivy Border
4330	Fairy	As 4230
4331 to 4345	Fairy	Ivy Border (Rd 175636)
4346	Fairy	Sunflower & Leaf Border

November 1891

4347	Worcester Breakfast	Badge
4348	Fairy	Sunflower & Leaf Border
4349 to 4350	Fairy	Jungle Sheet
4351 to 4352	Lily	Jungle Sheet
4353	Fairy	Bramble
4354 to 4355	Lily	Jungle Sheet
4356 to 4357	Alex	Gold Sprigs
4358 to 4361	Victoria Breakfast	Chain Border
4362 to 4363	Lily	Jungle Sheet
4364	Daisy	Ivy
4365 to 4369	-	Not used
4370 to 4377	Fairy, Daisy	Border Pattern
4378 to 4379	Fairy, Daisy	Gold Chrysanthemum, as 4301
4380 to 4579	-	Not used
4580	Alex	Dresden Flowers - enamalled

January 1892

4581	Gladstone Breakfast	Badge
4582 to 4590	Shell	Stippled Colours
4591	-	Not used
4592 to 4598	Shell	Inside Colours
4599 to 4604	-	Not used
4605 to 4610	Alex, Fairy	Inside Colours
4611 to 4617	-	Not used
4618	Sweets	Dresden Flowers
4619	Fairy	Dresden Flowers

February 1892

4620 to 4621	Worcester Breakfast	Badge
4622	Victoria Breakfast	Badge
4623	Fairy, Daisy, Empire	Dresden Flowers - enamalled
4624	Sweets	Dresden Flowers - enamalled
4625 to 4626	Fairy	Dresden Flowers - enamalled
4627	Sweets	Dresden Flowers - enamalled

March 1892

4628	Silver	Badge
4629	Alex	Gold Edge
4630	Daisy	Chrysanthemum
4631 to 4642	Victoria	Jungle Sheet
4643 to 4645	-	Not used
4646 to 4651	Lily	Ivy Border (seconds), special order
4652	Alex	As 4346
4653	Daisy	Jungle Sheet

May 1892

4654	Roman Breakfast	Badge
4655	Gladstone Breakfast	Badge (seconds)
4656	Butter, Muffins etc	Badge
4657	Lily	Margarette, as 3875
4658 to 4659	Alex	Outside Colour
4660	Fairy	Jungle Sheet

102

September 1892

4661	Minton Irish	Badge	

November 1892

4662	Gladstone	Badge	
4663 to 4668	Shell	Outside Colour	
4669	Paris	Badge	

December 1892

4670	Victoria Breakfast	Badge	
4671 to 4682	Victoria	Sunflower Border	
4683 to 4686	-	Not used	
4687	Minton Irish	Badge	
4688	-	Not used	
4689	May	Japan - blue, as 3690	

May 1893

4690	Victoria Milk & Muffin	Badge	
4691 to 4704	Fairy	Ivy Border	
4705 to 4706	-	Not used	
4707 to 4709	Daisy	Jungle Sheet	
4710	Victoria	Badge	
4711 to 4724	Lily	Kensington Print	
4725	-	Not used	
4726	Lily	Kensington Print	
4727	-	Not used	
4728	Roman	Badge	
4729	Paris Irish	Badge	
4730	Minton Irish	Badge	
4731 to 4742	Victoria	Wild Flowers	
4743 to 4747	-	Not used	
4748	Victoria	Badge	
4749 to 4750	-	Not used	
4751 to 4763	Daisy	Basket Of Flowers	
4764 to 4769	-	Not used	
4770 to 4779	Shell	Shaded Ground	
4780	Fairy	Flower Print - enamalled	
4781	May	Flower print - enamalled	
4782	Fairy	Flower Print - enamalled	
4783 to 4784	May	Flower Print - enamalled	
4785	May	Daisy Print (not sold)	
4786 to 4790	-	Not used	
4791 to 4802	Fairy	Basket Of Flowers (seconds)	
4803 to 4806	-	Not used	
4807 to 4810	Daisy	Shaded Ground	
4811 to 4822	Victoria	Ivy Border	
4823 to 4826	-	Not used	
4827	Daisy	Shaded Ground	
4828	Shell	Shaded Ground	
4829 to 4830	-	Not used	
4831 to 4843	May	Ivy Border	
4844 to 4850	-	Not used	
4851 to 4862	May	Jungle Sheet	
4863 to 4870	-	Not used	
4871 to 4882	Fairy	Ivy Border (seconds)	
4883 to 4890	-	Not used	
4891 to 4902	Fairy	Star Border	
4903 to 4910	-	Not used	
4911 to 4927	Daisy, Empire	Ivy Pattern	
4928 to 4930	-	Not used	
4931 to 4945	May	Lace Border	
4946 to 4950	-	Not used	
4951 to 4962	May	Lace Border, burnished gold	
4963 to 4970	-	Not used	
4971 to 4985	Empire	Fern decoration (Rd 213327)	
4986 to 4990	-	Not used	

June 1893

4991 to 5004	Roman	Lace Border	
5005 to 5010	-	Not used	
5011 to 5012	Fairy	Buttercups - enamalled	
5013 to 5016	-	Not used	
5017 to 5018	Fairy	Buttercups - enamalled	
5019 to 5021	-	Not used	
5022 to 5030	Lily	Kensington Pattern	

103

5031	–	Not used
5032 to 5035	Daisy	Basket Of Flowers
5036 to 5041	–	Not used
5042 to 5045	Empire	Ivy Print (Rd 175836)
5046 to 5051	–	Not used
5052	Fairy	Ivy Print, autumnal tints
5053	May	Lace Border, autumnal tints
5054	Fairy	Star Border, autumnal tints
5055	Shell	Ground Colour, autumnal tints
5056 to 5057	–	Not used
5058	Empire	Ground Colour
5059 to 5060	–	Not used
5061	Empire	Shaded Ground
5062 to 5064	–	Not used
5065 to 5066	Empire	Daisy Spray
5067	Empire	Ground Colour, autumnal tints
5068	Empire, Daisy, Fairy	Ivy print
5069	–	Not used
5070	Empire	Wreath Border
5071 to 5073	Fairy	Rococo Ornament
5074 to 5075	–	Not used
5076	May	Clover - enamalled
5077	Fairy	Poppies - enamalled
5078 to 5079	Lily	Roses - enamalled
5080 to 5081	Fairy	Poppies - enamalled
5082 to 5083	–	Not used
5084 to 5085	Lily	Roses - enamalled
5086	Daisy, Empire	Ivy Print, autumnal tints
5087 to 5090	Fairy	Ivy Print, shaded
5091 to 5106	Lily	Ivy Print
5107 to 5110	–	Not used
5111	Daisy	Poppies - enamalled
5112 to 5116, 5117	Lily	Sunflower (seconds), special order
5118	–	Not used
5119 to 5123	Daisy, Empire	Shaded Ground
5124 to 5125	Daisy	Shaded Ground
5126 to 5130	–	Not used
5131 to 5134	Empire	Shaded ground
5135	–	Not used
5135	Victoria	Fern Border, as 4245

5136	Lily	Fern Border, as 4245
5137	Shell	Ivy Print, shaded (Rd 175836)
5138	Daisy	Blackberries
5139	Empire	Shaded Ground
5140	Fairy	Sunflower & Leaf Border, as 4346
5141 to 5143	Empire	As 6531

April 1894

5144	Victoria Breakfast	Badge
5145 to 5146	Minton Breakfast	Badge
5147 to 5150	–	Not used
5151 to 5164	Empire	Rococo Ornament
5165 to 5170	–	Not used
5171 to 5185	Daisy	Blackberries (Rd 233180)
5186 to 5190	–	Not used
5191 to 5195	Daisy, Century	Shaded ground
5196 to 5199	–	Not used

May 1894

5200	Victoria	Badge
5201	–	Not used
5202 to 5205	Daisy	Blackberries
5206 to 5209	Rococo Jardiniere	Shaded Ground, special order
5210	–	Not used
5211 to 5225	Foley	Daisies Print
5226 to 5231	–	Not used
5232	Lily	Fern Border, as 5136
5233	Empire	As 6594
5234	Empire	As 6125

July 1894

5235	Victoria Breakfast	As 3480
5236	–	Not used

August 1894

5237	Worcester, Gladstone	Badge
5238 to 5242	Foley, Globe Jugs	Shaded Ground
5243 to 5258	Daisy, Foley, Empire	Plain Ground
	Dainty, Snowdrop	
5259 to 5261	-	Not used
5262 to 5265	Empire	Ivy Pattern
5266 to 5270	-	Not used
5271	Globe Jugs	Peony
5272 to 5276	-	Not used
5277	Globe Jugs	Plain Colour
5278 to 5279	-	Not used
5280	Globe Jugs	Plain Colour
5281	-	Not used
5282	Globe Jugs	Plain Colour
5283 to 5290	-	Not used
5291 to 5300	Alex, Daisy, Empire	Plain Ground
	Fairy	
5301	-	Not used

September 1894

5302	Victoria Breakfast	Badge
5303 to 5304	Daisy, Alex	Jungle Print (seconds)
5305	May	Badge
5306	-	Not used

November 1894

5307	Silver Breakfast, Badge	
	Gladstone	
5308	Lily, Fairy	Chrysanthemum - enamalled
5309	Lily, Fairy	Poppies - enamalled
5310	Lily	Poppies - enamalled
5311	Fairy	Poppies - enamalled
5312 to 5315	Fairy	Ivy Print, shaded
5316 to 5321	-	Not used
5322	Empire, Daisy	As 6172
5323 to 5338	Daisy, Foley, Empire	Plain ground
	Alex	

5339 to 5350	-	Not used
5351 to 5365	Shell	Plain Colours
5366 to 5371	-	Not used
5372 to 5380	Foley	Stippled Colours, as 4582
5381 to 5387	-	Not used
5388	Lily	Daisy print - enamalled
5389	Lily	Chrysanthemum - enamalled
5390	Lily	Poppies - enamalled
5391	Lily	Roses - enamalled
5392	Lily	Clover - enamalled
5393	Lily	Berries - enamalled

December 1894

5394	Gladstone, Worcester	Badge

February 1895

5395	Gladstone Breakfast	Badge
5396	Egg	As 3891

May 1895

5397	Paris Irish	Badge
5398	Worcester	Ivy Print
5399 to 5401	-	Not used
5402 to 5405	Daisy	Shaded Ground
5406 to 5411	-	Not used
5412	York, Egg	Ivy Pattern
5413 to 5415	Egg	Ivy Pattern
5416 to 5421	-	Not used
5422 to 5424	Foley, Globe Jugs	Garland Of Roses, as 6796
5425 to 5428	-	Not used
5429 to 5430	Foley, Empire	As 6605
5431	Daisy	Japan, as 6211
5432	Empire, Globe &	Special order
	Foley Jugs	
5433	Globe & Foley Jugs	Shaded Ground
5434 to 5443	-	Not used

105

June 1895

5444	Victoria	Badge

July 1895

5445	Victoria	Badge

August 1895

5446	Victoria	Badge

October 1895

5447	Minton	Badge
5448	Silver Breakfast	Badge
5449	Empire	As 6531
5450	-	Not used
5451 to 5464	York, Egg	Floral Spray with Scroll
5465 to 5471	-	Not used
5472 to 5475	York	Floral Spray with Scroll
5476 to 5482	-	Not used
5483	Foley	Daisies, as 6803
5484 to 5485	-	Not used
5486 to 5493	Foley	Shaded Ground
5494 to 5505	-	Not used
5506 to 5514	Foley	Shaded Ground
5515 to 5525	-	Not used
5526 to 5533	Fancy Articles	Shaded Upwards, as 6566
5534 to 5547	-	Not used
5548 to 5555	Foley Jugs	Shaded Upwards
5556 to 5568	-	Not used
5569 to 5588	Fancy Articles	Plain Ground
5589 to 5603	-	Not used
5604 to 5610	Daisy, Empire	Ivy Print, shaded
5611 to 5614	-	Not used
5615 to 5621	York	Shaded Ground (USA only)
5622 to 5625	Century	Trailing Violets Print (Rd 270002)
5626 to 5630	-	Not used
5631 to 5645	Century	Trailing Violets Print (Rd 270002)
5646 to 5650	-	Not used
5651 to 5663	Century	Trailing Violets Print (Rd 270002)
5664 to 5665	-	Not used
5666	Century	Trailing Violets print (Rd 270002)
5667 to 5670	-	Not used
5671 to 5685	Dainty Coffees	Daisy Border Pattern
5686 to 5690	-	Not used

December 1895

5691	Gladstone	Badge
5692	Century	Trailing Violets Print - enamalled

January 1896

5693	York	Roses & Forget-me-not Border
5694	York	Ornamental Border Pattern
5695	York	Ivy Print
5696	Century	Ivy Print
5697 to 5699	Empire, Daisy	As 6842
5700	Century	Chrysanthemum - enamalled
5701	Empire	Chrysanthemum - enamalled
5702 to 5705	Century	Ivy Pattern
5706 to 5709	-	Not used
5710	York, Egg	Holland Pattern
5711 to 5712	York	Keswick Pattern
5713	Empire, Daisy	As 6842
5714	Daisy	As 6846
5715	Daisy	Violet Print, as 6829
5716 to 5720	York	Shaded Ground (USA only)
5721	Snowdrop	As 6905
5722	Snowdrop	Daisy Clusters Print
5723	Empire	Daisy Clusters Print
5724	Gladstone Breakfast	Badge

April 1896

5725 to 5728	Empire	As 6172
5729	Century	Dresden Print, as 6875
5730 to 5735	Daisy	Plain Ground

Nos	Pattern	Notes
5736 to 5739	Trinkets	As 6867
5740 to 5741	-	Not used

June 1896

Nos	Pattern	Notes
5742	Victoria	Badge
5743	York	Shaded Ground
5744	Gladstone Breakfast	Badge
5745	Minton	Badge
5746 to 5748	Empire	As 6125
5749 to 5750	Foley	As 6795
5751 to 5752	Foley	As 6605
5753	Foley	Poppy - enamalled
5754	Empire, Daisy	As 5322
5755 to 5763	Dainty	Shaded ground
5764	-	Not used

September 1896

Nos	Pattern	Notes
5765	Minton	Badge
5766 to 5769	Daisy	As 6903
5770	-	Not used
5771 to 5785	Century	Ivy Pattern (seconds)
5786 to 5790	-	Not used
5791 to 5802	Empire	As 6904
5803 to 5810	Snowdrop	As 6905
5811	-	Not used
5812 to 5815	Snowdrop	Cameo Print (Rd 283973)
5816 to 5820	-	Not used
5821 to 5823	Snowdrop	Cameo print (Rd 283973)
5824 to 5831	-	Not used
5832 to 5836	Empire	Daisy Clusters print
5837 to 5841	-	Not used
5842 to 5845	Century	Surrey Scenery Print
5846 to 5850	-	Not used
5851 to 5852	Century	Surrey Scenery Print
5853	-	Not used
5854	Century	Surrey Scenery Print
5855 to 5856	-	Not used
5857 to 5860	Century	Surrey Scenery Print

Nos	Pattern	Notes
5861 to 5870	-	Not used
5871	Empire	Ivy Print
5872	Foley	Poppy Print - enamalled
5873 to 5882	Dainty	Shaded Ground
5883 to 5885	-	Not used

October 1896

Nos	Pattern	Notes
5886	Worcester Coffees	Badge
5887	Empire	Badge

November 1896

Nos	Pattern	Notes
5888	Victoria	Badge

December 1896

Nos	Pattern	Notes
5889	York	Badge
5890	-	Not used
5891 to 5894	Lily	Fern Print (Rd 276279)
5895	-	Not used
5896 to 5900	Lily	Fern print (Rd 276279)
5901	-	Not used
5902	Lily	Fern print (Rd 276279)
5903 to 5904	-	Not used
5905 to 5906	Lily	Fern Print (Rd 276279)
5907 to 5910	-	Not used
5911 to 5912	Empire	Daisy Clusters print
5913	-	Not used
5914	Empire	Daisy Clusters print
5915 to 5916	-	Not used
5917 to 5920	Empire	Daisy Clusters Print
5921	-	Not used
5922	Empire	Daisy Clusters Print
5923 to 5930	-	Not used
5931 to 5932	Snowdrop	Cameo Print
5933	-	Not used
5934	Snowdrop	Cameo Print
5935 to 5936	-	Not used
5937 to 5940	Snowdrop	Cameo print

5941	-	Not used
5942	Snowdrop	Cameo Print
5943 to 5944	-	Not used
5945 to 5946	Snowdrop	Cameo print
5947 to 5950	-	Not used
5951	Dainty	As 6922, enamalled
5952 to 5955	Lily, Royal	Fern Print
5956 to 5960	-	Not used

January 1897

5961 to 5964	Shakespeare Jugs	Not used
5965 to 5970	-	Badge
5971 to 5973	Silver Breakfast	Badge
5974	Roman	As 6839
5975	Daisy, Empire	Golden Green Print - enamalled
5976	Rococo Flower Pots	As 6894
5977	Rose Bowls	As 6925
5978 to 5979	Snowdrop	Not used
5980	-	Trailing Violets Print
5981	Lily	Not used
5982 to 5983	-	Trailing Violets Print
5984	Lily	Not used
5985 to 5986	-	Trailing Violets print
5987 to 5990	Lily	Not used
5991	-	Trailing Violets Print
5992	Lily	Not used
5993	-	Trailing Violets Print
5994	Lily	Not used
5995	-	Trailing Violets Print

July 1897

5996	Century	Flowers with Scroll Border
5997	Foley	Badge
5998	Roman	Badge
5999	Crinkled Flower Pots	As 6934
6000	Victoria	Badge

October 1897

6001	Dainty	Ivy Print
9002	Dainty	As 6811
9003	Dainty	Poppy, as 5753 - enamalled

November 1897

9004	Minton	Badge
9005	Dainty	As 5875
9006	Empire, Foley	As 6506
9007 to 9010	Crinkled Flower Pots	Shaded Ground
9011 to 9028	Dainty	Star Design, Cluster of Flowers
9029 to 9031	-	Not used
9032 to 9035	Dainty	Star Design, Cluster of Flowers
9036 to 9041	Sweets, Ash Trays etc	Shaded Ground
9042 to 9043	-	Not used
9044	Empire	Cluster of Daisies
9045	Crinkled Flower Pots	As 6934
9046 to 9049	-	Not used
9050	Snowdrop Bouillons	As 5805
9051	Snowdrop Bouillons	As 5809
9052 to 9059	Snowdrop, Dainty	Trailing Violets Print, as 5622
9060 to 9061	-	Not used
9062 to 9065	Dainty	Daisies Print (seconds)
9066	Century	Surrey Scenery
9067	Snowdrop	Daisies Print
9068	Roman	Daisies - enamalled

May 1898

9069 to 9075	Alex	Badge
9076	Dainty	As 9002
9077	Dainty	Star Design, Cluster of Flowers

July 1898

9078	Roman Breakfast	Badge (seconds)
9079	Roman	Daisies - enamalled

September 1898

9080	Chocolate Cup		Badge
9081	Roman		Badge (seconds)
9082	Lily		Fern Print

October 1898

9083	Snowdrop, Dainty		Chrysanthemum Print - enamalled
9084	Snowdrop		Chrysanthemum
9085	Beer Pulls		As 6974
9086	Gladstone Breakfast		Badge
9087	Beer Pulls		As 6978
9088 to 9091	Crinkled Flower Pots		Single Shade
9092 to 9096	-		Not used
9097 to 9100	Snowdrop		As 6994

April 1899

9101	Roman		Badge (seconds)
9102 to 9109	Empire		Floral Print with Scroll Border
9110 to 9114	-		Not used
9115	Empire		Floral print with Scroll Border
9116	New Fairy		Japan, as 6663, in blue
9117	New Fairy		Japan, as 4326, in blue
9118	Daisy		As 6031, enamalled in blue
9119	Daisy		Japan, as 6887, in blue
9120	Snowdrop		As 6929, enamalled in blue
9121	Violet		Surrey Scenery
9122	Violet		Fern Print, as 6897 (Rd 276279)
9123	Fancy Articles		As 4346
9124	Beer Pulls		As 6995
9125	Beer Pulls		As 6996
9126	Victoria Creams		Badge
9127	Violet		As 4346 (Rd 181135)
9128	Mugs		Japan, as 3942, in blue (Rd 84175)
9129	Flower Holder (Lapgeria)		As 7000
9130	-		Not used
9131 to 9145	New Fairy		Sprays of Poppies (Rd 331957)

9146 to 9150	-	Snowdrop	Not used
9151 to 9164	-	Snowdrop	Petunia Design (Rd 331956)
9165	-	Snowdrop	Not used
9166	-	Snowdrop	Petunia Design (Rd 331956)
9167 to 9170	-	Daisy	Not used
9171 to 9186	-	Flower Holder	Snowdrops (Rd 331958)
9187 to 9190	-	Flower Holder	Not used
9191 to 9192	-	Snowdrop	As 7000
9193	-	Empire	As 7045
9194 to 9195	-	Snowdrop	As 6172
9196 to 9197	-	Worcester	As 7045
9198	-	Lily	Badge
9199	-	Lily	Fern Print, as 6897

July 1899

9200		Worcester	Badge

August 1899

9201		Victoria Items	Badge
9202		Violet	As 6901
9203		Gladstone Breakfast	Badge

May 1900

9204		Silver	Badge
9205 to 9210		-	Not used
9211 to 9228		Foley	Roses Border Print
9229 to 9230		-	Not used
9231 to 9250		New York	Storks print
9251 to 9253		Silver, Gladstone	Bands
9254 to 9255		Snowdrop	As 9083
9256		Snowdrop	As 6994
9257		Roseberry Dessert	As 7041
9258		Century	As 7044
9259 to 9260		Snowdrop	As 7064
9261		Violet	As 5692
9262		Beer handles	As 6978
9263		Crinkled Fern Pots	As 6935
9264		Gladstone	Badge

109

December 1900

9265	Gladstone Breakfast	Badge
9266	Worcester	Badge
9267 to 9269	Empire	As 6172

January 1901

9270 to 9273	Fancy Articles	Plain Colours
9274 to 9278	-	Not used
9279 to 9282	Dainty	Daisy Border
9283 to 9286	-	Not used
9287	Daisy	Snowdrops
9288	-	Not used
9289	Empire	Floral Print, as 9106
9290	-	Not used
9291 to 9308	Gainsborough	Basket of Flowers (Rd 368024)
9309 to 9310	-	Not used
9311 to 9328	Lily	Dresden Flowers
9329 to 9330	-	Not used
9331 to 9335	Snowdrop	Cameo Print (Rd 283973)
9336 to 9338	-	Not used
9339	Empire	Daisies - enamalled as 6948
9340	Snowdrop	Daisies - enamalled as 6948
9341	Snowdrop	Thistle - enamalled as 7108
9342	Daisy	Violets - enamalled as 5715
9343	Dainty	Poppy - enamalled as 9003
9344	Empire	Chrysanthemum - enamalled as 6892
9345	Snowdrop	Stylised Flower & Stem, as 7069
9346	Snowdrop	As 6905
9347 to 9350	Empire	As 6842
9351 to 9368	Violet	Carnations & Border (Rd 354780)
9369 to 9469	-	Not used
9470	Victoria	Badge
9471	New York	Stork Print

February 1901

9472	Gainsborough	Badge
9473	Victoria	Badge
9474	Foley	Roses Print, as 9218

March 1901

9475	Victoria Creams	Badge
9476 to 9477	Beer Handles	Rose & Thistle - enamalled

April 1901

9478	Worcester, Silver Breakfast	Badge

May 1901

9479	Victoria	Badge
9480	Silver Breakfast	Badge
9481	Roman	Badge
9482	Empire	As 6842
9483	New York	Margarette, as 3873
9484	Empire	As 6842
9485 to 9487	Foley	Shaded Half Down
9488 to 9490	Lily	Shaded Half Down
9491 to 9493	Daisy	Shaded Half Down
9494 to 9496	Dainty	Shaded Half Down
9497 to 9499	Snowdrop	Shaded Half Down
9500 to 9502	Violet	Shaded Half Down
9503 to 9505	Empire	Shaded Half Down
9506	Dainty	Shaded Ground
9507	Trinkets	Solid Ground
9508 to 9510	Gem Hats	As 7211
9511	Gainsborough	As 7073

August 1901

9512	Dainty	Dresden Sprays - enamalled
9513	Gainsborough	As 7236
9514 to 9516	Gainsborough	As 7238 (9515 - enamalled)

September 1901

9517	Roman	Badge
9518	Gainsborough	Japan, as 7074
9519	Lily	As 9138
9520	Lily	As 9366
9521 to 9522	Lily	Daisies, as 9058
9523	Lily	Daisies, shaded, as 6805
9524	Lily	Daisies, as 5217
9525	Lily	Japanese Border Print

November 1901

9526	Gladstone, Globe Jugs	Badge

December 1901

9527	Silver, Globe Jugs	Badge
9528	Silver	Badge
9529	Empire	As 6842
9530	8" & 10" Plates	As 7126

January 1902

9531	Victoria Breakfast	Badge
9532	Victoria	Badge
9533 to 9536	Violet	Wild Rose Sprays (seconds)

February 1902

9537	Roman	Badge
9538 to 9541	Daisy	Daisy Border (seconds)
9542	Dainty	Badge

March 1902

9543	Dainty	Badge
9544	Gladstone	Badge
9545	-	Cancelled
9546	Worcester	Badge

9547 to 9548	New York	Badge
9549 to 9551	Alex	Badge

April 1902

9552	Roman	Badge
9553	New York	Stork Print, as 9471
9554	Roman	Badge
9555 to 9556	Bath Sets	Border Pattern, as 7346
9557	Bath Sets	Border Pattern, as 7347
9558 to 9561	Bath Sets	Daisy Border Pattern, as 7349
9562	Bath Sets	Daisies, Violets etc, as 6922
9563 to 9565	Bath Sets	As 7346

May 1902

9566	New York	Badge
9567	-	Cancelled

July 1902

9568	Gladstone	Badge
9569 to 9572	Crinkled Flower Pots	Shaded Ground

September 1902

9573	Silver	Badge
9574 to 9575	Bath Sets	As 7345

October 1902

9576	Roman	Badge

November 1902

9577	Muffin Dish	Badge
9578	York	Badge
9579	Roman Breakfast	Badge
9580	Rosebury Dessert	Jungle Print, as 6021
9581	Gainsborough	Roses, as 7447

Number	Pattern	Description
9582 to 9584	Gainsborough, Royal	As 7294
9585	Royal	As 6172
9586 to 9587	Dainty	Shaded Ground
9588	Victoria	Badge
9589	Silver	Badge
9590 to 9591	Gainsborough	Roses, as 7447
9592 to 9593	Victoria	Oak Leaf Border
9594	Dainty	Shaded Ground, as 5873
9595	Dainty	Shaded Ground, as 5761
9596 to 9599	Violet	As 9351
9600 to 9602	-	Not used
9603 to 9606	Lily	Wild Rose Sprays
9607 to 9610	-	Not used
9611 to 9630	Royal	Coloured Fiber
9631 to 9633	Snowdrop	Carnation
9634	Lily	Badge
9635	Royal	As 7580
9636 to 9638	Snowdrop	Lilac
9639 to 9640	-	Not used
9641 to 9643	Dainty	Double Poppy
9644 to 9645	-	Not used
9646 to 9648	Violet	Old Chrysanthemum
9649 to 9650	-	Not used
9651 to 9653	Violet	Dandelion
9654 to 9655	Royal	Blue Fiber
9656	Royal	As 7466
9657	Royal	Dresden Flowers, as 6192
9658	Royal	Indian Tree - enamalled, as 7479
9659	Royal	As 7424
9660	Royal	As 7425
9661	-	Not used
9662 to 9665	Violet	Wild Roses Print (seconds)
9666 to 9680	Dainty, Antique	Plain Ground

March 1903

Number	Pattern	Description
9681	Minton Irish	Badge

April 1903

Number	Pattern	Description
9682	Gladstone	Badge
9683	Royal	As 9585

May 1903

Number	Pattern	Description
9684	Silver	Badge
9685	Roman	Badge
9686	Teapots, Coffee Pots	Badge

June 1903

Number	Pattern	Description
9687	Worcester Breakfast	Badge

July 1903

Number	Pattern	Description
9688	Roman Breakfast	Badge
9689 to 9690	Victoria, Lily, Roman, etc	Badge
9691 to 9709	Royal	Lily Prints with Rings (Rd 40405)
9710 to 9714	-	Not used
9715 to 9716	Violet	Daisy Border, as 9506
9717	New York	As 9596
9718	New York	As 9599
9719 to 9722	Bath Sets	Forget-me-not Border, as 7552
9723 to 9724	-	Not used
9725	Gainsborough	Anemones, as 7365
9726 to 9727	8" Gainsborough Plate	Fishnet Border, Star Centre, as 7499
9728 to 9730	Daisy Sugar & Cream	Shaded Colours
9731 to 9732	-	Not Used
9733	Silver	Badge

August 1903

Number	Pattern	Description
9734	New York	Badge
9735	Royal	As 9691
9736	Gainsborough	Roses - enamalled
9737 to 9738	Dainty	Daisies
9739	Dainty	Clover - enamalled

112

November 1903

9740	Silver Breakfast	Badge
9741	Dainty	Chrysanthemum
9742	Dainty	Cornflower
9743	Dainty	Violets
9744	Daisy	Violets
9745	Worcester Breakfast	Badge
9746 to 9748	Daisy	Floral Print with Scroll, as 9106
9749	Snowdrop	As 5658
9750	Bath Sets	As 7349
9751	Bath Sets	As 7348
9752	Bath Sets	As 7346
9753	American Salad Bowl	Indian Tree, as 9658
9754	American Salad Bowl	Floral Wreath & Roses, as 7715
9755	Dainty	Floral Sprays - litho (seconds)
9756	Daisy	Floral Sprays - litho (seconds)
9757	Foley	Floral Sprays - litho (seconds)
9758	Lily	Floral Sprays - litho (seconds)

December 1903

9759	Royal	Badge
9760	Royal	Forget-me-not & Maiden Fern, as 7686
9761	Dainty, Gainsborough	Rose Pansy, as 7335
9762	Dainty	Clover, as 7677
9763	American Salad Bowl	Wreaths & Roses, as 7598
9764	Gainsborough	Blue Japan, as 6888
9765	Royal	As 7643
9766	Royal	Red Japan, as 4253
9767	Silver	Badge
9768	Roman Breakfast	Badge
9769	Roman	Badge
9770	Victoria	Badge
9771 to 9790	Violet	Chain Border Design
9791 to 9810	Foley	Grass Print
9811 to 9830	Lily	Floral sprays & Scroll (Rd 331959)
9831 to 9850	Dainty	Anemones Print
9851 to 9869	Daisy	Sprays & Border Design, (Rd 425157)

January 1904

9870	Daisy	Sprays & Border Design, (Rd 425157)

March 1904

9871	Roseberry Tall Comports	Badge
9872	Foley	Japan, as 7019, special gilt, (Rd 3931)

April 1904

9873	Roman	Badge
9874 to 9876	Gainsborough	Goblins, as 7762
9877	Violet	As 9811

June 1904

9878	Silver	Badge
9879	New York	Badge
9880	Jonquil Lamps	Shaded
9881	Royal	Badge
9882	Royal	Festoon Roses, as 7733
9883 to 9884	Card Holder	Allan Mail Steamers
9885	Royal Coffees	Rose Sprays, as 7238

July 1904

9886	York	Badge
9887	Mug	Badge
9888 to 9889	Turkish Cans	Japan

August 1904

9890	Turkish Cans	As 7006

113

September 1904

9891	Roman	Badge
9892	Foley	Rose Sprays, as 7447
9893 to 9894	Dainty	Festoon Roses, as 7733
9895	Dainty	Shaded Ground, as 5875

December 1904

9896	Worcester	Badge
9897	Royal	Anemones, as 7367
9898	Dainty	As 9666
9899 to 9901	Dainty	Plain Grounds (seconds)
9902 to 9905	Violet	As 9102 (seconds)
9906	Royal	Japan, as 7188 (Rd 3931)
9907	Foley Flute	Floral Sprigs, litho, as 9756
9908	Foley Flute	Floral Sprigs, litho, as 9755
9909	Lily	Floral Sprigs, litho, as 9757
9910	Foley Flute	Floral Sprigs, litho, as 9757
9911 to 9930	Foley Flute	Border Violet Print
9931	-	Not used
9932 to 9935	Gainsborough	Basket of Flowers

January 1905

9936	Worcester Coffees	Badge
9937	Dainty	Primula - enamalled
9938	Gladstone	Badge

March 1905

9939	Hammersley Breakfast	Badge

April 1905

9940	Roman	Badge
9941	Gladstone	Badge

May 1905

9942	Victoria Creams	Badge
9943	Gladstone	Badge
9944	Royal, Foley Flute	As 9758
9945	Royal, Foley Flute	Rose Sprays, litho

June 1905

9946	Gladstone Breakfast	Badge
9947	Royal	Wreath with Roses, as 7598
9948	Victoria	Oak Leaf Pattern, as 9592

August 1905

9949	Silver Breakfast	Badge
9950	Minton Irish	Badge
9951 to 9952	Victoria	Oak Leaf Pattern, as 9592
9953 to 9955	-	Not used

September 1905

9956	Victoria	Badge
9957	New York	Badge
9958	Gladstone	Badge
9959	Worcester Breakfast	Badge
9960	Royal Breakfast Set	Badge
9961 to 9964	Victoria	Daisies, as 9056
9965 to 9968	Victoria	Floral Sprays, as 9102
9969 to 9972	Victoria	Anemones, as 9831
9973 to 9978	Victoria	Ivy Border
9979 to 9980	-	Not used
9981 to 9986	Victoria	Chain Border Design, as 9771
9987 to 9988	-	Not used
9989 to 9994	Victoria	Grass Print, as 9791
9995 to 9997	-	Not used

November 1905

9998	Gladstone	Badge
9999	Victoria Breakfast	Badge
10000	Old York	Badge

December 1905

10001	Gladstone	Badge
10002 to 5	Lily	Rose Sprays
10006 to 7	-	Not used

February 1906

10008	New York	Badge
10009	Gladstone	Badge
10010	Roman	Badge
10011 to 30	Antique (Square)	Floral Garland Border
10031 to 50	Lily	Rose Sprays (Rd 468736)
10051 to 70	Court	Floral Chains
10071 to 90	Devonshire	Rose Sprays with Scroll Border
10091 to 92	Royal	As 7818
10093	Royal	As 7072
10094	Royal	As 7779
10095	Royal	As 7279
10096 to 98	Royal	As 7690
10099 to 101	-	Not used
10102 to 103	Gainsborough	As 7424
10104	Duplex Sweet, Cake Tray	White & Gold

March 1906

10105	Victoria	Badge
10106	Gainsborough	Roses, as 7447
10107	Gainsborough	Wild Roses, as 7866
10108	Lily	Daisies, as 9961
10109 to 111	Royal	As 7818
10112 to 113	Royal, Foley Flute	Banded

May 1906

10114	Dainty	Roses, as 7447
10115	Royal	Rose Festoon & Bows, as 7733
10116	Roman	Badge

June 1906

10117	Victoria Creams	Badge
10118	Worcester	Badge
10119	Roco Dessert	As 7591
10120	Plain Horns	Badge
10121	Gladstone	Badge
10122 to 125	Royal, Foley Flute	Floral Sprays, as 9102 (seconds)

July 1906

10126	Lily	Clover Leaf (seconds)
10127	Foley Flute	Clover Leaf (seconds)
10128	Lily	Clover Leaf (seconds)
10129 to 130	Ash Trays	Badge
10131	Royal	Badge
10132 to 135	Gainsborough	Daisies, as 9506 (seconds)
10136	Gainsborough	Wreaths with Roses, litho
10137	Court	Clusters of Roses, litho
10138	Royal, Foley Flute	Floral Wreath, litho

August 1906

10139	New York	Badge
10140	Gainsborough	As 7819
10141	Old Quaint Jugs	As 7216
10142 to 144	Royal	As 7086
10145 to 146	Royal	As 7812
10147	Royal	As 7691
10148	Gainsborough	As 7474
10149 to 150	Royal	As 7815
10151	Royal	As 7693
10152	Royal	As 7660
10153	Gainsborough	As 7558

10154	Royal	As 7294
10155	Royal	As 7538
10156	Royal	As 9127 (Rd 181135)
10157	Gainsborough	As 7798
10158	Gainsborough	As 7612
10159	Royal	As 7693
10160 to 163	Snowdrop	Jungle Print

December 1906

10164	Old York	Badge
10165	Quaint Jug	As 7220
10166	Old York	Badge
10167	New Low Lily	Floral Sprays, litho
10168	New York	Violets
10169	Dorothy	Japan, as 3464 (Rd 3931)
10170	Royal	As 7508
10171 to 172	10" Gainsborough Plate	As 7541
10173 to 175	10" Gainsborough Plate	As 7918
10176 to 177	Royal	As 7937
10178	Dorothy	Japan, as 4023
10179 to 180		Not used

January 1907

10181	Edinburgh Breakfast	Badge

February 1907

10182	Victoria	Badge
10183	New York Jugs	Badge
10184	Dainty Jugs	Badge

March 1907

10185	Gladstone	Badge
10186	Victoria	Badge
10187	Dorothy	Delphic Sunset, as 7332

April 1907

10188	Sick Feeders	Badge
10189	New York Breakfast	Badge
10190	Minton	Badge
10191 to 210	New Low Lily	Wreath with Rose Chain (Rd 496830)
10211 to 230	Dorothy	Rose Bloom & Chains with Scroll
10231	Dorothy	As 7984
10232	Worcester Breakfast	Badge
10233	Snowdrop	Jungle Print

May 1907

10234	Victoria	Badge
10235	Gainsborough	As 7283

June 1907

10236	Plain Horns	Badge
10237	Gainsborough	As 7930
10238	China	Fathers Of Empire, as 7376 (Rd 407992)
10239	Dorothy	As 7929
10240	Royal	Cornflower, as 7685
10241	Royal	As 7951
10242	Bute	Wreath of Roses, litho, as 7956
10243	Royal	As 7951
10244	Dorothy	Margarette, as 3873
10245	New York	Floral Wreath, litho, as 10138

September 1907

10246	Silver Breakfast	Badge
10247	Roseberry Dessert	Roses, litho, as 7852
10248	On China	Oleander Spray - enamalled
10249	On China	Life Plant - enamalled

October 1907

10250	Worcester Breakfast	Badge
10251	New York	As 10113
10252	Gladstone	Badge
10253	Dorothy	Wisteria, litho
10254 to 259	Gainsborough	Plain Ground

November 1907

10260 to 266	Antique	Plain Ground
10267	-	Not used

December 1907

10268	Large Open Breakfast	Badge (special order)
10269 to 270	10" Plain	As 8025
10271 to 272	-	Not used
10273	Silver Breakfast	Badge

January 1908

10274	New York	Badge
10275	Bute	Chain Border, litho
10276	10" Plain	As 7598
10277	Royal, Foley Flute	As 10112
10278 to 279	Royal	As 8061
10280 to 281	Gainsborough	As 8062
10282	Royal, Foley Flute	Plain Edge Line
10283	Royal, 10" Plain	As 7970
10284 to 285	Bute	Shamrock, as 8064
10286 to 288	Mugs	Badge
10289	Gainsborough	Rose Festoon, as 7952
10290	Bute	Banded Edge, as 8039

April 1908

10291	Gladstone	Badge

May 1908

10292 to 295	Low Lily	As 10191 (seconds)
10296	New York	Badge

June 1908

10297 to 299	New York	Badge
10300	New York	As 10137
10301	Victoria	As 10253
10302 to 305	Dorothy	As 10211 (seconds)
10306	Double Handle Cups	Badge
10307	-	Not used
10308	Dainty	Wisteria, litho
10309 to 310	Bute	Shamrock, as 8064
10311	Bute	As 8024
10312	10" Plain	As 7973
10313	Bute	Shamrock, as 8064
10314 to 315	-	Not used
10316	Victoria	Litho, as 10137
10317	Victoria	Litho, as 10245
10318	Dainty	Roses & Daisy Festooned, litho
10319	Bute	As 8070

September 1908

10320	Roman	Badge
10321	Bute	As 8038
10322	Plates	As 7952

October 1908

10323	New York	Badge
10324 to 327	Dainty	Shaded Ground
10328	Plates	As 7951
10329	New York	As 10251
10330	Plates	Badge
10331	Gainsborough, 10" Plate	As 8062
10332	Gainsborough, Bute	As 8021

117

10333	Gainsborough	Star Border, litho	
10334	Dorothy	Badge	

November 1908

10335	Edinburgh	Badge	
10336	Bute	Wisteria, litho	
10337	Gainsborough	Roses & Ribbon Border, as 7976	
10338 to 340	Gainsborough	Poppies, as 7584	
10341	Royal	As 8110	
10342	Gainsborough	Rose Spray	
10343 to 346	Dorothy	As 8132	
10347	Gainsborough	Green Key & Rose Border, litho	
10348 to 349	Gainsborough	As 8140	

January 1909

10350	Worcester	As 10231	
10351	Dorothy	As 10318	
10352 to 353	Vases & Gems		
10354	Bute	As 8133	
10355	Royal	As 8106	
10356	New York	As 10333	
		As 8094	

April 1909

10357	New York	Badge	
10358	Sick Feeders	As 10357	
10359	New York	As 10318	
10360	New York	As 9758	
10361	New York	As 10167	
10362	Bute	As 8064	
10363	Dorothy	As 10333	
10364	New York	As 10333	
10365	Royal	Wisteria, as 10253	
10366	Royal	As 10347	
10367	Bute	As 10333	

May 1909

10368	New York	Badge	As 10137
10369	Dorothy		

June 1909

10370	New York Coffees	Indian Tree, as 9658	
10371	New York Coffees	As 7598	
10372	New York Coffees	As 7969	
10373	Victoria	As 7970	
10374	Victoria	As 7581	
10375	Bute	As 10137	
10376	Victoria	Badge	
10377	Victoria Creams, China etc	Badge	
10378 to 380	China Gems	As 8177	
10381 to 382		Not used	
10383 to 385	China Gems	As 8178	
10386	New York	Badge	
10387	Roseberry Dessert	As 8165	
10388	Snowdrop	As 10137	
10389	Dainty	Clusters Print, as 5918	
10390	Dainty	Ivy, as 5045	
10391	Gainsborough	As 9937	
10392	Gainsborough	Wisteria, as 10253	
10393	New York	As 10277	

August 1909

10394	Victoria	Badge	
10395	Empire Sugar & Creams	As 8097	
10396	Gainsborough	As 10351	
10397	Bute	Rose & Shamrock Border (seconds)	
10398	Dorothy	Rose & Shamrock Border (seconds)	
10399	Gainsborough	As 3891	
10400	Unhandled Coffee	Wreath, litho	
10401	Unhandled Coffee	Roses	
10402	Unhandled Coffee	Banded, as 7982	

10403	Unhandled Coffee	Ribbon Band	
10404	Dorothy	As 8192	
10405	New York	Wisteria, as 10253	
10406	New York	As 8063	
10407	New York	As 10347	
10408	Dainty	As 8121	
10409	New York	As 8070	
10410	Dorothy	As 9947	
10411	New York	As 8064	
10412	China	Seaside Subject - enamalled	
10413	Bute	Swallow Print, blue	
10414	Royal	As 8064 (seconds)	
10415	Dainty	As 8064 (seconds)	
10416	Lily Breakfast	As 10253 (seconds)	
10417	Bute	Vine Border, as 8070 (seconds)	
10418	Roman	Vine Border, as 8070 (seconds)	
10419	Royal	As 8110	

November 1909

10420	New York	Badge	
10421	Ideal Sweets	Autumnal Tints	
10422 to 423	Ideal Sweets	Plain Ground	
10424	Souffle	Plain Ground	
10425	Violet Breakfast	As 8064 (seconds)	
10426	Unhandled Coffee	As 10318	
10427	Unhandled Coffee	As 10347	
10428	Bute	As 10138	
10429	Gainsborough	Vine Border, as 8070 (seconds)	
10430	Dorothy	Vine Border, as 8070	
10431	Royal	As 8243	
10432 to 433	Gainsborough	As 8126 - enamalled	
10434	Gainsborough	As 10347 (seconds - Australia)	

December 1909

10435	Dainty	As 10318 (seconds - Australia)	
10436	Gainsborough	As 8126	
10437	Bute	As 10333 (seconds - Australia)	
10438	Roman	As 10253 (seconds - Australia)	

1890

6002 to 6006	Lily	Sprig Decoration, panelled
6007 to 6014	Lily	Border Pattern
6015 to 6020	Lily	Border Pattern, panelled
6021 to 6027	Daisy	Jungle Print (Rd 117220)
6028	Lily	Chrysanthemum
6029	Lily	Convolvulus
6030	Daisy	Japan - Derby Pattern, red & black
6031	Daisy	Daisy Wreath print (Rd 118300)
6032 to 6036	Lily	Convolvulus
6037	–	Not used
6038 to 6040	Lily	Chrysanthemum
6041 to 6043	–	Not used
6044 to 6047	Lily	Border Print
6048 to 6049	–	Not used
6050	Lily	Border Print
6051 to 6059	Lily	Sunflower
6060 to 6061	Daisy	Panelled Decoration
6062	Lily	Panelled Decoration
6063	Lily	Border Decoration
6064 to 6067	Lily	Convolvulus
6068	–	Not used
6069 to 6070	Lily	Chrysanthemum
6071 to 6074	–	Not used
6075	Daisy	Japan - blue & red (Rd 118301)
6076	Daisy	Birds Nest Design
6077	Lily	Birds Nest Design
6078	Worcester	Daisy Wreath, as 6031
6079	Lily	Convolvulus
6080 to 6084	Dessert	Flowering Reed
6085	Dessert	Convolvulus
6086 to 6087	Dessert	Flowering Reed
6088	Daisy	Jungle print (Rd 117220)
6089	–	Not used
6090 to 6094	Daisy	Gold Sprig Decoration, panelled
6095 to 6099	Daisy	Convolvulus
6100 to 6101	–	Not used
6102 to 6104	Lily	Sprig Border Design
6105	Lily	Convolvulus

6106 to 6110	Daisy	Flowering Reed	6192	Daisy	Dresden Flowers - enamelled
6111 to 6112	-	Not used	6193 to 6201	Daisy	Dresden Flowers
6113 to 6115	Dessert	Plain Ground	6202 to 6205	-	Not used
6116 to 6118	-	Not used	6206	Daisy	Dresden Flowers - enamelled
6119 to 6121	Dessert	Plain Ground	6207 to 6208	-	Not used
6122 to 6124	-	Not used	6209 to 6210	Daisy	Sprig Border
6125 to 6127	Daisy	Diamond Design	6211	Daisy	Japan, as 6030
6128	Daisy	Flowers	6212	Daisy	Japan - red & gold
6129	Daisy	Folded Panel Design	6213	Lily	Japan - red & gold
6130	Daisy	Buttercups - enamelled	6214	Daisy	Sprigs, as 3719
6131	Lily	Buttercups - enamelled	6215 to 6219	Daisy	Rococo Design
6132	Dessert	Flowers	6220 to 6221	Daisy	As 6210
6133	Daisy	Buttercups (Rd 133642)	6222 to 6223	Daisy	Rococo Design, stippled gold
6134	Lily	Buttercups (Rd 133642)	6224	Daisy	As 6091, stippled gold
6135 to 6136	Daisy	Buttercups (Rd 133642)	6225	Daisy	As 6092, stippled gold
6137 to 6142	-	Not used	6226	Daisy	As 6094, stippled gold
6143 to 6152	Lily	Lace Border Design	6227	Daisy	As 6216, stippled gold
6153	-	Not used	6228	Daisy	As 6173, stippled gold
6154 to 6157	Lily	Lace Border Design	6229	Daisy	As 6218, stippled gold
6158 to 6160	-	Not used	6230	Daisy	As 6217, stippled gold
6161	Lily	Lace Border Design	6231 to 6242	Daisy	Paradise Print (Rd 164516)
6162 to 6165	Daisy	Gold Sprigs	6243 to 6245	-	Not used
6166 to 6168	Lily	Gold Sprigs	6246	Daisy	As 6210, stippled gold
6169	Lily	Japan - blue, red & gold	6247	Daisy	As 6220, stippled gold
6170 to 6171	Daisy	Jungle print (Rd 117220)	6248	Daisy	As 6221, stippled gold
6172 to 6173	Daisy	Rococo Design in Gold print	6249	Daisy	As 6219, stippled gold
6174 to 6175	Daisy	Rose Branches	6250	Daisy	As 6186, stippled gold
6176 to 6178	Daisy	Rococo Design in Gold Print	6251 to 6262	Lily	New Daisy Border
6179	Lily	Rococo Design in Gold print	6263 to 6265	-	Not used
6180	Daisy	As 6162	6266	Daisy	As 6188, stippled gold
6181 to 6183	Daisy	Rococo Design	6267 to 6270	Daisy	As 6210
6184	Daisy	Flowering Reed, as 6107	6271 to 6282	Victoria	New Daisy Border
6185	Lily	Sunflower Print	6283 to 6285	-	Not used
6186 to 6188	Daisy	Rococo Design	6286 to 6287	Daisy	Jungle Print
			6288	Daisy Muffin	As 6172, gold star
April 1890			6289	Daisy Muffin	As 6210
			6290	Daisy	As 6172, stippled gold
6189	Lily	Sunflower Print	6291	Daisy	As 6209
6190	Daisy	Gold Sprigs, panelled	6292	Daisy	As 6172
6191	Daisy	Gold Sprig Border	6293 to 6294	Daisy	As 6209

6295	Daisy	Daisy Print	6352	Dessert	Orchid & Bird, shaded
6296 to 6301	Daisy	As 6061	6353	Dessert	Floral Group
6302 to 6305	Daisy	As 6125	6354	Dessert	Ivy, Moss & Birds
6306 to 6307	Daisy	As 6295	6355	Dessert	Spray of Phlox & Bird
6308	Daisy	As 6210	6356	Dessert	Spray of Hop
6309 to 6310	Daisy	As 6209	6357	Dessert	Daisies
6311	Daisy	Daisies - enamalled & shaded	6358	Dessert	Sprays with Butterflies
6312	Daisy	Hawthorn Flowers - enamalled	6359	Dessert	Border Pattern
6313	Daisy	Gold Decoration	6360	Dessert	Ivy & Geranium Flowers
6314	Daisy, Court	Shell Design, panelled & shaded	6361	Dessert	Fir Cone & Foliage
6315	Daisy	Fir Cones & Foliage, shaded	6362	Dessert	Heather & Butterflies
6316	Daisy	Fir Cones & Foliage, shaded	6363	Dessert	Sprays of Nuts
6317	Fairy	Violet Stems, shaded	6364	Dessert	Wild Rose & Butterflies
6318	Fairy	Ivy Leaves & Berries, shaded	6365	Dessert	Ragged Robin & Daisies
6319	Fairy	Gold Border design, shaded	6366	Dessert	Strawberry & Butterfly
6320	Fairy	Fir Cones & Foliage, shaded	6367	Dessert	Festoons, Roses & Forget-me-nots
6321	Fairy	Fern & Flower Sprays, shaded	6368	Dessert	Japan - enamalled in black
6322	Fairy	Jasmine Flowers, shaded	6369 to 6374	Dessert	Japan
6323	Shell	Shaded Colours	6375	Dessert	Japan (Rd 3931)
6324 to 6325	Shell	Ivy Print, shaded colours	6376	Dessert	Japan
6326	Daisy	Hawthorn Blossom, shaded	6377	Dessert	As 6325
6327	Daisy, Court	Hawthorn Blossom, shaded	6378 to 6379	Dessert	Wild Roses, Ferns & Landscape
6328	Daisy	Strawberries, shaded	6380		Not used
6329	Fairy	Hawthorn Blossom, shaded	6381	Dessert	Strawberry & Maiden Hair Ferns
6330	Fairy	Peach Blossom, shaded	6382	Dessert	Blackberry, Butterflies & Ferns
6331	Daisy	Flower Design at edge, panelled	6383	Dessert	Game Birds with Daisies - enamalled
6332 to 6333	Daisy	Plum Blossom	6384	Dessert	Fern Border
6334	Daisy	As 6315	6385 to 6386	Dessert	Sprays of Double Roses
6335	Fairy	As 6315	6387	Dessert	Fir Tree & Storks
6336 to 6338	Fairy	Dresden Flowers (Rd 157867)	6388	Dessert	Painted Landscape
6339	Shell	Flower Spray & Dragonfly, shaded	6389	Dessert	Landscaped, Bird & Daisy Panels
6340 to 6341	Fairy	Decorative Border	6390	Dessert	As 6348, shaded
6342	Fairy	Branches with Berries	6391	Dessert	As 6385, only Wild Roses, shaded
6343 to 6344	Fairy	Decorative Border	6392	Dessert	As 6386, only Double Roses, shaded
6345	Fairy	Daisies & Ferns, shaded	6393	Dessert	Wild Rose, shaded
6346	Shell	Primrose & Forget-me-nots, shaded	6394	Dessert	Double Rose, shaded
6347	Daisy	Daisies, shaded	6395 to 6396	Dessert	Printed Landscape, blue band
6348 to 6349	Shell	Flower Spray Print, shaded	6397	Dessert	Peach Blossom & Fruit
6350	Dessert	Wisteria Sprays, shaded	6398	Dessert	Blossom & Fern
6351	Dessert	Ivy, Geraniums & Forget-me-nots			

6399 to 6400	Dessert	As 6357		6477	Shell	As 6324
6401 to 6403	Dessert	Jasmine		6478	Victoria	Spray
6404 to 6405	Dessert	As 6172		6479	Fairy	Roses
6406	Fairy	As 6327		6480	Fairy	Sprays
6407	Trinket	Rococo; Red Japan		6481	Fairy	Daisies
6408	Dessert	Stork & Daisies		6482	Fairy	
6409 to 6412	Rococo Jardiniere etc	Shaded Ground		6483	Fairy	Jasmine
6413 to 6414	-	Not used				
6415 to 6417	Rococo Jardiniere etc	Shaded Ground		**May 1893**		
6418 to 6420	-	Not used				
6421	Roseberry Dessert			6484	Empire	As 6324
6422 to 6424	Fairy	Festooned Rose Print		6485	Empire	As 6325
6425 to 6429	-	Not used		6486	Empire	As 6377
6430 to 6431	Trinket	Rococo Design		6487	Empire	As 6477
6432	Trinket	Ivy & Stems		6488		Not used
6433 to 6435	Daisy	As 6311		6489	Daisy	As 6436
6436 to 6438	Daisy	Heath Border		6490	Fairy	As 6436
6439 to 6441	Fairy	As 6340		6491	Trinkets	As 6431
6442	Dessert	As 6360		6492	Daisy	Michaelmas Daisies
6443 to 6446	-	Not used		6493 to 6495	May	Daisies - enamalled
6447	Dessert	As 6354		6496	Shell	Daisies - enamalled
6448 to 6451	-	Not used		6497	Daisy	Michaelmas Daisies - enamalled
6452	Trinkets	Flower Sprays		6498	May	Michaelmas Daisies - enamalled
6453	Trinkets	Daffodils		6499	Daisy	Daisies
6454	Trinkets	Festoon of Roses		6500	-	Not used
6455	Dessert	Small Groups of Flowers & Fruit		6501	May	Daisies - enamalled
6456	Dessert	Fir Cones, Stems & Foliage		6502	Luncheon Trays	Wild Rose
6457	Dessert	Printed Roses		6503	May	Daisies
6458	Dessert	Sea View with Bird		6504 to 6505	May	Michaelmas Daisies - enamalled
6459	Dessert	Storks & Tree		6506 to 6514	Empire, May, Foley	
6460	Dessert	Landscape with Sprigs of Flowers		6515	Dessert	
6461	Dessert	Birds, Plants & Grasses		6516 to 6517	Daisy	
6462	Trinket Sets	Shaded Ground		6518 to 6520	Dessert	
6463 to 6466	Trinket Sets	Jungle Sheet		6521 to 6523	Empire	
6467	Trinket Sets	Roses		6524 to 6529	-	Not used
6468 to 6470	Dessert	As 6327		6530	May	
6471	May	Japan, as 3632		6531	Empire	
6472 to 6474	Shell	Sprays of Flowers		6532 to 6533	Daisy	
6475	Shell	As 6099		6534 to 6535	Trinket	Poppy
6476	Shell	As 6342		6536	Trinket	Bands

122

6537	Trinket	Rococo Flowers
6538 to 6540	Dessert	Poppies
6541	Dessert	
6542 to 6547	Empire	Not used
6548 to 6552	-	As 6295
6553	Daisy	Dresden Flowers - enamalled
6554	Rococo Jardiniere etc	
6555 to 6556	Rococo Jardiniere etc	Not used
6557 to 6558	-	
6559 to 6561	Rococo Jardiniere etc	Not used
6562 to 6563	-	As 6531
6564 to 6565	Empire	Shaded Downwards
6566 to 6571	Rococo Jardiniere etc	
6572 to 6577	Dessert	
6578 to 6579	Trinket Sets	Not used
6580 to 6587	Shell	
6588 to 6589	-	
6590 to 6593	Trinket Sets	Not used
6594 to 6596	Empire	
6597 to 6599	Foley	
6600 to 6603	-	Not used
6604	Foley	
6605	Foley, Empire	
6606 to 6611	Foley	
6612 to 6617	Empire	
6618 to 6620	Foley	
6621 to 6624	Empire	
6625	Foley Fish Plate	
6626 to 6629	Foley Game Plate	
6630	Foley Fish Plate	
6631 to 6635	Foley Dinnerware	
6636 to 6639	Foley Muffins	
6640	Foley Dinnerware	
6641 to 6656	Foley Fish Plate	
6657 to 6661	Foley Dinnerware	

July 1894

6662	Daisy	
6663	Fairy	Japan
6664	Dessert, Cake Stand	Japan - blue, red & gold
6665	Globe Jugs	
6666 to 6667	Fairy	
6668	Lily	
6669	Fairy	
6670	Foley Dinnerware	
6671 to 6676	Foley	
6677	-	Not used
6678 to 6688	Foley	
6689 to 6690	Fancy Articles	Not used
6691 to 6712	-	
6713	Fairy	
6714 to 6715	Foley	
6716	Rococo Tea Caddies	Not used
6717 to 6720	-	
6721	Rococo Tea Caddies	Not used
6722 to 6725	-	
6726	Plain Tea Caddies	
6727	Foley, Dainty Jugs	
6728 to 6731	Foley	
6732 to 6735	-	Not used
6736 to 6738	Empire	
6739 to 6742	-	Not used
6743 to 6745	Foley	
6746 to 6749	-	Not used
6750 to 6757	Foley Jugs	
6758 to 6759	-	Not used
6760 to 6762	Foley Dinnerware	
6763 to 6766	-	Not used
6767 to 6771	Foley Dinnerware	
6772 to 6775	-	Not used
6776 to 6779	-	Cancelled
6780 to 6784	-	Not used
6785	Foley	
6786 to 6794	-	Not used
6795 to 6798	Foley	
6799 to 6801	-	Not used
6802 to 6805	Foley	
6806 to 6810	-	Not used
6811	Foley, Daisy	

123

June 1895

6812	Roseberry Dessert	
6813	Victoria, Lily	As 3719
6814	Victoria, Lily	As 3714
6815	Victoria, Lily	As 3582
6816	Victoria, Lily	As 3581
6817	York, Egg	Rococo Ornament
6818 to 6819	-	Not used
6820	Empire	As 6172
6821 to 6822	Empire, Daisy	As 6172
6823 to 6826	-	Not used
6827	Fairy	
6828	Empire	As 6605
6829 to 6831	Daisy	Violets
6832	Daisy	
6833 to 6834	Century	
6835 to 6840	Daisy	
6841 to 6842	Empire, Daisy	Panelled Gold Border Decoration
6843	Daisy	Panelled Gold Border Decoration

October 1895

6844 to 6847	Daisy	Panelled Gold Border Decoration
6848	Century	Poppy, as 5310
6849	Century	Chrysanthemum - enamalled
6850 to 6851	Century	Dresden Flowers - enamalled
6852	Century	Poppy - enamalled
6853	Daisy	Garland of Flowers & Ornament
6854	Daisy	As 6845
6855 to 6856	Century	Dresden Flowers
6857	Daisy	Garland of Flowers & Ornament
6858 to 6859	Dainty	Shaded Ground
6860	Dainty	Solid Ground
6861 to 6862	Poppy	Shaded Ground
6863	Poppy	Autumnal Tints
6864 to 6866	Century	Chrysanthemum
6867	Trinkets	Shaded Ground
6868	Foley	Poppy Print
6869	Dainty	

6870	Poppy	Gold Border Design
6871 to 6872	Dainty	Japan, as 6663
6873	Century	Dresden Groups
6874	Century	Dresden Groups
6875	Century, Royal	Poppy - enamalled
6876	Foley	Forget-me-nots
6877	Foley	As 6811
6878	Foley	Violets - enamalled
6879	Empire	Violets - enamalled
6880	Daisy	Violets - enamalled
6881	Century	Daisy Clusters
6882	Century	Kensington Print
6883	Empire	As 6865
6884	Foley	Kensington Print
6885	Lily	Kensington Print - enamalled
6886	Lily	Japan, black & red
6887	Daisy	Japan, blue
6888	Empire	Plain ground
6889	Empire, Foley	
6890	Crinkled Salads	
6891 to 6893	Empire	Chrysanthemum
6894 to 6895	Rose Bowl	
6896	Rose Bowl, Salads etc	Shaded Grounds
6897	Century	Fern Print (Rd 276279)
6898	Trinkets	Red Japan, as 6407
6899	Rose Bowl	Shaded Ground

September 1896

6900	Dessert	Japan - blue, red & gold, as 6664
6901	Century	Blue Scenery
6902	Rose Bowl etc	Plain Ground
6903	Daisy	Diamonds & Shields with gold design
6904	Empire	Gold Sprigs & Leaf Design
6905	Snowdrop	Gold Scroll & Leaf Design, panelled
6906	Trinkets	Shaded Ground
6907 to 6908	Century	Surrey Scenery - enamalled
6909 to 6910	Century	Fern Print (Rd 276279)
6911 to 6912	Snowdrop	Cameo - enamalled

6913	-	Not used
6914	Empire	Daisy Cluster (Rd 283662)
6915	-	Not used
6916 to 6917	Empire	Daisy Cluster (Rd 283662)
6918 to 6919	Century	Fern Print
6920 to 6922	Dainty	Mixed Single Flower Pattern
6923 to 6928	Snowdrop	Rose with Small Flowers in Panels
6929	Snowdrop	Chrysanthemum
6930 to 6931	Shakespeare Jugs	
6932	Rococo Teapot	
6933	Roseberry Dessert	
6934 to 6935	Crinkled Flower Pot	
6936 to 6937	Snowdrop	Poppy
6938	Crinkled Flower Pots	
6939 to 6940	Snowdrop	Poppy - enamalled
6941 to 6943	Snowdrop	Lilac - enamalled
6944 to 6947	Snowdrop	Poppy (Rd 306302)
6948 to 6949	Empire	Trailing Violets Print (Rd 270002)
6950	Snowdrop	Japan, black & red
6951	Hair Tidies	Stippled Gold on White
6952	Oval Shells	Plain Ground
6953	Hair Tidies	Plain Ground

May 1898

6954	Snowdrop	Shamrock - enamalled
6955	Duplex Sweets	Plain Ground
6956	Snowdrop	Thistle
6957	Desserts	Daisy Clusters
6958	Desserts	Large Daisies
6959	Desserts	Daisy Clusters
6960	Desserts	Figures Transfer
6961	Empire	Orchids, litho
6962	Dainty	Roses & Snowdrops, litho
6963	Lily	Roses, litho
6964	Rococo Lamp	Daisy Clusters
6965	Rococo Candle Holder	
6966 to 6967	Rococo Lamp	
6968 to 6969	Bamboo Lamp	
6970	Crinkled Lamp	

6971	Jonquil Lamp	
6972	Bamboo Lamp	
6973	Jonquil Lamp	
6974	Dainty	Chrysanthemums - enamalled
6975	Beer Pulls	
6976	Rococo Lamp	
6977	Jonquil Lamp	
6978	Rococo Lamp	
6978A	Beer Pulls	
6979 to 6980	Dainty	Japan - enamalled
6981	Snowdrop	Japan, blue & red
6982	Daisy	Japan, blue & red (Rd 119505)
6983 to 6988	Snowdrop	Japanese Rose
6989	Daisy	Chrysanthemum
6990	Toast Rack	
6991	Bamboo Lamp	
6992	Rococo Lamp	
6993	Square Sweets	
6994	Snowdrop	Star Design
6995 to 6996	Beer Pulls	
6997	Crinkled Lamp	
6998	Snowdrop	Japan, blue & red

February 1899

6999	Lamp & Stand	
7000	Flower Holder	
7001	Flower Tubes	
7002	Crinkled Flower Holders	
7003	Fern Pots	
7004	Turkish Cans	Japan, as 3464
7005	Turkish Cans	Japan, blue, as 4247
7006	Turkish Cans	
7007	Thistle Horns	
7008 to 7017	-	Cancelled
7018	Snowdrop	Thistle
7019	Foley	Japan, as 3464 (Rd 3931)
7020	Dessert	Japan, as 6998
7021	Dessert	Japan, as 9119
7022 to 7024	Crinkled Flower Pot	

Number	Pattern		Number	Pattern	
7025 to 7032	-	Not used	7132 to 7136	Century	Iona Abbey
7033 to 7038	Snowdrop		7137 to 7146	Gainsborough	Tinte Abbey
7039 to 7040	Trinkets		7147	Century	Woodcock
7041	Roseberry Desserts		7148 to 7150	Gainsborough	Peacock
7042 to 7043	Snowdrop		7151	Globe Jugs	Prairie Hen
7044	Century		7152	Gainsborough	Roach
7045	Snowdrop		7153 to 7154	Roseberry Dessert	Iona Abbey
7046	Century		7155 to 7156	Roseberry Dessert	Tinte Abbey
7047 to 7052	Rococo Trinkets		7157	8" Gainsborough Plate	Woodcock
7053	-	Not used	7158	8" Gainsborough Plate	Peacock
7054 to 7058	Rococo Trinkets		7159	8" Gainsborough Plate	Prairie Hen
7059 to 7062	Beer Pulls		7160	8" Gainsborough Plate	Roach
7063	Lily Breakfast		7161	8" Gainsborough Plate	Perch
7064	Snowdrop		7162	Roseberry Dessert	Ross Castle
7065	Daisy		7163	Roseberry Dessert	
7066	Foley		7164	10" Century Plate	Perch
			7165	10" Gainsborough Plate	Ptarmigan
September 1900			7166	10" Gainsborough Plate	Trout
7067	Victoria	Badge	7167	10" Gainsborough Plate	Star Centre
7068	Violet		7168 to 7169	Roseberry Dessert	Peacock
7069	Snowdrop	Petunia Design (Rd 331956)	7170 to 7171	Roseberry Dessert	Star Centre
7070	Century		7172	Roseberry Dessert	Perch
7071	Beer Handles		7173	10" Century Plate	Partridge
7072 to 7073	Gainsborough		7174 to 7175	Gainsborough Dessert	Pheasant
7074	Gainsborough	Japan	7176 to 7183	Gainsborough Dessert	
7075	Gainsborough		7184	Gainsborough Dessert	Japan, as 4255
7076	Foley		7185 to 7186	Gainsborough Dessert	Japan, as 4247
7077	Gainsborough Dinner		7187	Gainsborough Dessert	
7078 to 7080	Roseberry Dessert		7188	Gainsborough Dessert	Japan (Rd 3931)
7081 to 7082	Century		7189	Gainsborough Dessert	
7083 to 7085	Gainsborough		7190 to 7192	Gainsborough Dessert	Daisy Head Border
7086 to 7094	Century		7193 to 7194	Gainsborough Dessert	Double Leaf Border
7095	Gainsborough		7195 to 7197	10" Gainsborough Plate	Cornflower Print
7096 to 7100	Century		7198 to 7200	Roseberry Dessert	
7101 to 7121	Gainsborough		7201	Dessert Jug	Landscape
7122	Century		7202	Dessert Jug	Fish
7123	Gainsborough, Globe Jug		7203	Dessert Jug	Game
7124	Globe Jug		7204	Gems - 20	
7125 to 7131	Gainsborough		7205	Gems - 21	
			7206	Gems - 22	

126

7207	Gems - 26		7280	Gainsborough	As 7115
7208	Gems - 27		7281	Gainsborough	As 7118
7209	Gems - 28		7282	Gainsborough	
7210	Gems - 30		7283	Gainsborough	As 7146
7211	Gem Hats - 35		7284 to 7285	Gainsborough	As 7072
7212	Gems - 37		7286 to 7287	Gainsborough	As 7097
7213	Gems - 39		7288 to 7289	Gainsborough	As 7123
7214	Gems - 33		7290	Gainsborough	As 7116
7215	Gems - 24		7291	Gainsborough	As 7117
7216 to 7222	Old Jug		7292		Not used
7223	Gainsborough	Japan, blue, as 4255			
7224		Cancelled	**January 1902**		
7225 to 7229	Gainsborough		7293	Gainsborough	As 7122
7230	Gainsborough Muffin		7294	Gainsborough	As 7255
7231 to 7233	Gainsborough Dessert		7295 to 7296	Gainsborough Dessert	
7234	Old Jug		7297	Jug	
7235 to 7240	Gainsborough		7298 to 7299	Two Handled Jug	
7241 to 7243	Dinnerware	Farmyard Animals	7300	Jug	As 7115
7244 to 7247	Violet	Carnations & Floral Band	7301	Jug	As 7114
7248 to 7249	Gainsborough	Basket of Flowers - enamalled	7302 to 7303	Jug	As 7216
7250	Daisy	Snowdrops - enamalled	7304	Jug	As 7146
7251 to 7253	Old Jug	As 7216	7305	Jug	As 7093
7254	Foley Coffee	Blue Delph	7306 to 7308	Square B&B Plate	Rococo Panels with Flower Sprays
7255	Gainsborough	As 7088	7309	Two Handled Mug	
7256	Gainsborough	Carnations	7310	Gainsborough	As 7119
7257	Violet		7311	Bath Set	Pansy, Rose & Forget-me-not
7258	Gainsborough	As 7084	7312 to 7313	Gainsborough	As 7146
7259	8" Gainsborough Plate	As 7242	7314	Gainsborough	As 7119
7260	8" Gainsborough Plate	As 7158	7315 to 7317	Gainsborough Dessert	
7261 to 7265	Dessert		7318	Old Jug	Japan, as 6888
7266	8" Gainsborough Plate	As 7158	7319	Old Jug	As 7097
7267	Gainsborough	As 7125	7320	Century	As 7099
7268	Gainsborough	As 7126	7321 to 7324	Gainsborough	As 7238
7269	Gainsborough	As 7127	7325	Gainsborough	As 7077
7270 to 7271	Gainsborough	As 7125	7326 to 7327	Gainsborough	Small Cornflowers
7272 to 7275	Gainsborough	As 7108	7328	Gainsborough	Cornflowers
7276	Gainsborough	As 7148	7329 to 7330	Old Jug	Small Cornflowers
7277	Gainsborough	As 7095	7331	Square B&B Plate	
7278	Shakespeare Jugs		7332	China Pieces	Sunset Delphic
7279	Gainsborough				

7333	Gainsborough	Small Cornflowers	
7334	Gainsborough	As 7097	
7335	Gainsborough	As 7311	
7336	China Pieces	Green Delphic	
7337 to 7338	Rococo Dessert		
7339 to 7343	Dessert		
7344	Gainsborough	As 7093	
7345	Old Jug		
7346 to 7349	Bath Set		
7350	Square B&B Plate		
7351	Old Jug	As 7274	
7352 to 7353	Gainsborough Dessert		
7354 to 7355	Dessert		
7356	-	Not used	
7357 to 7358	Gainsborough	Small Cornflowers	
7359	Gainsborough	Cornflower Border	
7360 to 7362	Dessert	Welsh Rabbit Print	
7363 to 7368	Gainsborough	Anemones	
7369 to 7371	Square B&B Plate		
7372 to 7376	Gainsborough		
7377	Gainsborough	As 7093	
7378	Gainsborough	As 7094	
7379	Roseberry Dessert	As 7087	
7380	Dessert	Anemones	
7381	Dessert		
7382	Gainsborough Dessert	Anemones	
7383	Gainsborough Dessert	Carnation	
7384	Dessert		
7385	Dessert	As 6390	
7386 to 7387	Shakespeare Jug		
7388	Gainsborough	Carnation	
7389 to 7390	8" Plain Plate		
7391	10" Plain Plate		
7392	8" Plain Plate		
7393	8" Gainsborough Plate		
7394 to 7395	Dessert		
7396 to 7398	Roseberry Dessert	As 7162	
7399 to 7410	8" Gainsborough Plate		
7411	Gainsborough	Carnation	
7412 to 7413	Gainsborough	Cyclamen	
7414	Gainsborough Dessert	Cyclamen	
7415	Gainsborough	Cyclamen	
7416	Gainsborough	Carnation	
7417 to 7421	Gainsborough	Cyclamen	
7422	Crinkled Flower Pot		

March 1902

7423	Minton	Badge	
7424 to 7425	Gainsborough		
7426 to 7427	Dainty		
7428 to 7430	Foley		
7431	Dessert	Landscape	
7432	Dessert		
7433	Dessert	Swans	
7434	Dessert	Mountain Scene	
7435	Dessert	Red Grouse	
7436	Dessert		
7437 to 7439	Gainsborough Dessert		
7440	Dessert		
7441	Gainsborough	As 7114	
7442	Gainsborough	Dresden Flower	
7443 to 7446	Dainty		
7447	Gainsborough	Sprigs of Roses	
7448	Gainsborough		
7449	Gainsborough Dessert	Landscape with Castle	

September 1902

7450	Dessert		
7451	Square B&B Plate	As 7369	
7452	Gainsborough	As 7272	
7453	Bath Set	As 6922	
7454	Three Handled Mug	As 7309	
7455 to 7456	Three Handled Mug	As 7298	
7457	Square B&B Plate	As 7396	
7458	Rococo Dessert	As 7336	
7459 to 7460	Gainsborough Dessert		
7461	Gainsborough, Royal		
7462 to 7463	Royal	As 7238	

128

Number	Type	Description
7464	Chemists Jar	
7465	Royal Coffees	
7466	Royal	
7467	8" Plain Plate	
7468	8" Gainsborough Plate	
7469 to 7472	Royal Bouillons	
7473	8" Gainsborough Plate	
7474 to 7483	Royal	
7484	8" Gainsborough Plate	
7485	Water Set	
7486	Bath Set	
7487 to 7495	Royal	
7496	Gainsborough Dessert	
7497	Royal	(USA only)
7498	8" Plain Plate	
7499 to 7500	8" gainsborough Plate	
7501	Royal	
7502	8" Gainsborough Plate	Japan
7503	8" Gainsborough Plate	Flying Woodcocks - Micklewright
7504	8" Gainsborough Plate	Grouse on Moor - Micklewright
7505	8" Gainsborough Plate	Woodcocks in Glade - Micklewright
7506 to 7509	Royal	
7510	8" Gainsborough Plate	Gleaners - Rhead
7511	Royal	
7512	8" Gainsborough Plate	Old Songs - Alcock
7513	8" Gainsborough Plate	On The Temple Steps - Alcock
7514	8" Gainsborough Plate	The Months - Alcock
7515	8" Gainsborough Plate	The Seasons (Summer) - Alcock
7516	8" Gainsborough Plate	The Seasons (Winter) - Alcock
7517	8" Gainsborough Plate	Fair Women of 19th Century - Alcock
7518	8" Gainsborough Plate	Dolley Varden - Rhead
7519	Rococo Dessert	Dead Pheasant - Micklewright
7520 to 7521	Royal	
7522	8" Gainsborough Plate	Partridges & Chicks - Mussell
7523	8" Gainsborough Plate	Peacock - Mussell
7524	8" Gainsborough Plate	Trout - Mussell
7525	8" Gainsborough Plate	La France Rose - Mussell
7526	8" Gainsborough Plate	Amherst Pheasant - Mussell
7527	8" Gainsborough Plate	Orchids - Mussell
7528	8" Gainsborough Plate	Snipe - Micklewright
7529	8" Gainsborough Plate	Arundel Castle - Micklewright
7530	8" Gainsborough Plate	Morland Castle - Micklewright
7531	Rococo Dessert	Bream - Micklewright
7532 to 7533	8" Gainsborough Plate	Golden Carp - Micklewright
7534	8" Gainsborough Plate	Flying Partridge - Micklewright
7535	Rococo Dessert	Prairie Hens - Micklewright
7536	Gainsborough	Woodcocks
7537 to 7539	Royal	
7540	8" Gainsborough Plate	Modern Poets - Rhead
7541	10" Plain Plate	
7542	Royal	
7543	Boxes etc	
7544	Rococo Dessert	Sweet Pea
7545	Rococo Dessert	Wild Rose
7546 to 7547	Rococo Dessert	Potato Plants
7548	Rococo Dessert	Roses
7549	Rococo Dessert	Dresden Flowers
7550	Royal	
7551	8" Gainsborough Plate	
7552	Bath Set	
7553 to 7558	Royal	
7559	Gainsborough	
7560	8" Plain Plate	
7561 to 7562	8" Gainsborough Plate	
7563	Foley Teapots	
7564	Dessert	Japan, as 7074
7565 to 7566	Royal Jug	
7567 to 7574	10" Plain Plate	
7575	Royal	
7576	8" Gainsborough Plate	Old English Poets - Rhead
7577 to 7578	Royal Jug	
7579	Rococo Dessert	
7580 to 7581	Royal	
7582	Rococo Dessert	
7583	Dainty	
7584	Gainsborough	
7585 to 7590	8" Plain Plate	
7591	Rococo Dessert	Landscape
7592	Rococo Dessert	Fish

129

7593	Rococo Dessert	Lower Lake Villamey		7741	8" Gainsborough Plate	Fish (Perch) - New Series
7594	Rococo Dessert			7742	8" Plain Plate	Fish Subjects
7595 to 7597	Roseberry Dessert			7743 to 7745	Royal	
7598	Royal			7746	8" Gainsborough Plate	Great Masters (Turner) - Micklewright
7599 to 7601	Rococo Dessert			7747	8" Gainsborough Plate	Great Masters (Constable) - Micklewright
7602 to 7604	Roseberry Dessert			7748	8" Gainsborough Plate	Landscape
7605	Gainsborough			7749 to 7755	Royal	
7606	Rococo Dessert			7756	8" Gainsborough Plate	
7607 to 7611	8" Gainsborough Plate			7757 to 7761	Menu	
7612	Snowdrop			7762	Gainsborough	Goblins
7613	Royal			7763 to 7766	Royal	
7614	8" Gainsborough Plate			7767	Crinkled Lamp	
7615	Dainty			7768	Rococo Lamp	
7616	Roseberry Dessert			7769 to 7770	Royal	
7617	8" Gainsborough Plate			7771	8" Gainsborough Plate	
7618 to 7619	Royal			7772 to 7773	Royal	
7620 to 7621	Boxes, Creams etc			7774	Dainty	Primroses
7622 to 7624	Royal			7775	8" Plain Plate	
7625 to 7627	8" Plain Plate			7776 to 7777	Royal	
7628 to 7647	Royal			**June 1904**		
7648	8" Gainsborough Plate			7778 to 7782	Royal	
7649 to 7654	Royal			7783 to 7785	Gainsborough	
7655	-	Not used		7786	Royal	
7656 to 7663	Royal			7787	Menu	
7664	Bath Sets			7788	Royal	
7665 to 7715	Royal			7789	Gainsborough	
7716	Roman	(USA only)		**August 1904**		
7717 to 7718	New York	(USA only)		7790	Gainsborough	
7719 to 7722	Royal			7791	Royal	
7723	8" Gainsborough Plate	Peacocks - New Series		7792	Gainsborough	
7724 to 7727	Royal			7793	Royal Coffees	
7728	8" Gainsborough Plate	Grouse - Micklewright		7794	Royal	Japan
7729	8" Gainsborough Plate	Fish - Micklewright		7795	Rococo Dessert	
7730 to 7733	Royal			7796	Royal	
7734 to 7735	8" Plain Plate					
7736	8" Gainsborough Plate	Female Vignettes - Hewitt				
7737	8" Gainsborough Plate	Landscape				
7738	8" Gainsborough Plate	Landscape - Micklewright				
7739	8" Plain Plate					
7740	8" Gainsborough Plate	Landscape - Great Masters				

7797	Royal Breakfast		7884	Dainty	
7798 to 7805	Royal		7885 to 7886	Sick Feeders	
7806	Foley Flute		7887 to 7888	Rococo Desserts	
7807 to 7824	Royal		7889 to 7890	Antique	
7825	Gainsborough		7891	Devon	As 7804
7826	China Gems - 22		7892	Rococo Dessert	
7827	China Gems - 20		7893	Royal	
7828	China Gems - 24		7894	Royal, Foley Flute	As 7840
7829	China Gems - 21		7895	Devonshire	As 7880
7830	China Gems - 27		7896	New York	As 7839
7831	China Gems - 28		7897	New York	As 7840
7832	Royal	Japan	7898	Dainty	As 7884
7833	Royal		7899 to 7902	Royal	As 7119
7834	Menu		7903	Gainsborough	
7835 to 7837	Royal		7904 to 7905	Bath Sets	
7838	Royal Coffees		7906 to 7909	Royal	
7839 to 7840	Royal, Foley Flute		7910 to 7912	Antique	
7841	Royal		7913	Royal	
7842	Gainsborough		7914	Gainsborough	
7843	Square		7915 to 7917	Royal	
7844	Antique	Japan, blue & red	7918	10" Gainsborough Plate	
7845	Royal	Japan, blue & red	7919	Gainsborough	
7846	Royal	Japan	7920	Royal	
7847	Royal		7921 to 7922	10" Gainsborough Plate	
7848 to 7850	Roseberry Dessert		7923 to 7928	Dorothy	
7851	Devonshire		7929	-	Cancelled
7852 to 7860	Roseberry Dessert		7930	Gainsborough	
7861	Devonshire				
7862	Devonshire	Irises	**January 1907**		
7863 to 7864	Devonshire		7931	Angelic	
7865 to 7866	Gainsborough		7932	10" Plain Plate	
7867	Devonshire		7933	Gainsborough	
7868	Antique	Japan, blue & red	7934	Dorothy	
7869 to 7870	Roseberry Dessert		7935	New York	
7871 to 7873	Edward	Apple Blossom - enamalled	7936 to 7939	Royal	
7874 to 7877	Edward	Apple Blossom - tinted	7940	10" Gainsborough Plate	
7878	Empire, Court	Apple Blossom - gold	7941	Royal	
7880 to 7881	Gainsborough	As 6061	7942	10" Plain Plate	
7882 to 7883	Antique		7943	10" Gainsborough Plate	

131

7944 to 7945	Royal		8035	Bute	
7946 to 7947	10" Plain Plate		8036 to 8037	10" Plain Plate	
7948 to 7950	10" Gainsborough Plate		8038 to 8039	Bute	
7951 to 7952	10" Plain Plate		8040	Dainty	Roses, litho
7953 to 7955	10" Gainsborough Plate		8041 to 8043	10" Plain Plate	
7956	Royal		8044	Dorothy	Japan
7957	Gainsborough		8045	Low Lily	
7958	10" Plain Plate		8046 to 8050	10" Plain Plate	
7959 to 7961	10" Gainsborough Plate		8051 to 8052	Dorothy	
7962 to 7965	10" Plain Plate		8053 to 8054	Gainsborough	
7966	Royal		8055 to 8057	10" Plain Plate	
7967	10" & 8" Gainsborough Plate		8058	Royal, Foley Flute	
7968 to 7969	10" Plain Plate		8059 to 8060	10" Plain Plate	
7970	10" & 8" Plain Plate		8061	Royal	
7971	10" Gainsborough Plate		8062	Gainsborough	
7972	10" & 8" Plain Plate		8063	Dorothy	Rose Sprays, litho
7973	10" Gainsborough Plate		8064	Bute	Violets
7974	8" Gainsborough Plate		8065	10" Plain Plate	
7975	Royal		8066	Bute	
7976	10" Plain Plate		8067	10" Plain Plate	
7977	Dorothy	Peter Pan	8068	10" Plain Plate	Bourbon Borders with Roses
7978 to 7980	10" Plain Plate		8069	10" Plain Plate	
7981	Royal		8070	Bute	Vine Border
7982 to 7984	Dorothy		8071	10" Plain Plate	
7985 to 7990	10" Plain Plate		8072	10" Plain Plate	Rose Wreath
7991	Royal, Bute		8073 to 8074	10" Plain Plate	
7992 to 8011	10" Plain Plate		8075 to 8076	Royal	
8012	10" Gainsborough Plate		8077 to 8080	10" Plain Plate	
8013	10" Plain Plate		8081	Vases 1-17, Gems etc	Castles
8014 to 8015	Royal		8082	Vases 1-17, Gems etc	Yachting Scenes
8016	10" Plain Plate		8083	10" Plain Plate	Rose Sprays, litho
8017	Royal, Bute		8084	10" Plain Plate	
8018	Royal		8085	Bute	
8019	Fancies		8086	Royal	
8020	Royal		8087	Bute	
8021	Gainsborough		8088 to 8089	10" Plain Plate	
8022	Royal				
8023	10" Plain Plate				
8024	Bute				
8025 to 8034	10" Plain Plate				

June 1908

8090	10" Plain Plate	
8091	Worcester Breakfast	
8092	Dorothy	
8093	Royal	
8094	Bute	Rose, litho
8095	Gainsborough	Rose, litho
8096	Royal	
8097	Dorothy	
8098 to 8099	10" Plain Plate	
8100	Dorothy	As 7926
8101	Bute	
8102	10" Plain Plate	
8103 to 8104	Bute	
8105	10" Plain Plate	
8106	Bute	

October 1908

8107	10" Plain Plate	
8108	Royal	
8109	10" Plain Plate	
8110	Royal	
8111	Antique	
8112 to 8113	Snowdrop	
8114	Dainty	
8115	Bute	
8116 to 8117	Gainsborough	
8118	10" Plain Plate	
8119	Dainty	
8120	Snowdrop	
8121	Dainty	
8122	Antique	
8123 to 8124	Gainsborough	
8125	Snowdrop	
8126 to 8127	Gainsborough	

January 1909

8128 to 8129	Bute	Water Lilies
8130	Dorothy	
8131	Vases	
8132	Dorothy	
8133	China Vases & Gems	
8134 to 8139	10" Plain Plate	
8140 to 8141	Gainsborough	
8142 to 8147	10" Plain Plate	
8148	Gems	
8149 to 8150	China Sweets	
8151 to 8152	-	No Details
8153	Gainsborough	
8154 to 8162	10" Plain Plate	
8163	Gainsborough	
8164	Gainsborough	Japan, blue & red
8165 to 8167	Roseberry Desserts	
8168	Bute	
8169	Roseberry Dessert	
8170 to 8174	10" Plain Plate	
8175	Shell Fern Pot	
8176	Dorothy	
8177 to 8178	China Gems	
8179 to 8182	Roseberry Dessert	
8183	10" Plain Plate	
8184 to 8185	Ideal Cake	
8186 to 8187	Gems	Japan
8188	10" Plain Plate	
8189 to 8190	Bute	Blue Swallows
8191	Vases & Gems	Moonlight Decoration
8192	New York	
8193	Vases & Gems	
8194 to 8195	Bute	Blue Storks
8196 to 8197	Roseberry Dessert	
8198 to 8199	Square Sweets	
8200 to 8201	10" Plain Plate	
8202	Gainsborough	
8203 to 8204	Crinkled Round Sweets	
8205	Gainsborough	

133

8206	Crinkled Round Sweets	
8207	Boston Sweets	
8208	Crinkled Round Sweets	
8209	Royal	
8210	Crinkled Salads	
8211	Globe Honey	
8212 to 8214	Crinkled Salads	
8215 to 8216	Square Cake Plate	
8217	10" Plain Plate	
8218	Antique Teapot	

December 1909

8219	Royal	
8220 to 8224	10" Plain Plate	
8225	Royal	
8226 to 8235	10" Plain Plate	
8236	Royal	
8237 to 8239	10" Plain Plate	
8240 to 8242	Gainsborough	
8243	Square Cake Plate	
8244	Dorothy	
8245	Bute	
8246	Dorothy	
8247 to 8248	Bute	
8249	Gainsborough	
8250	Bute	
8251	Royal	
8252 to 8257	-	For USA - gold borders
8258	Bute	

March 1910

8259	Bute	
8260	Bath Set	
8261 to 8274	10" Plain Plate	
8275	Gainsborough	

July 1910

8276	Plain Cruet Set	
8277 to 8279	Crinkled Biscuit Jar	
8280 to 8281	Bute	
8282	10" Plain Plate	
8283	Crinkled Globe Honeys	
8284	New York	
8285 to 8287	Bute	
8288	Crinkled Biscuit Jar	
8289 to 8290	Victoria	
8291	Foley Flute	
8292	New York	
8293	Argyle	
8294	Gainsborough	Roses & Forget-me-nots, litho
8295	Dainty	Double Roses, litho
8296	Gainsborough	Louis Panel with Roses, litho
8297	Gainsborough	Bell Wreath with Roses
8298	Gainsborough	Key & Roses, litho
8299	Gainsborough	Ribbon & Roses, litho
8300	Gainsborough	Circles around Roses, litho
8301	Gainsborough	Festoons & Fruit
8302	Gainsborough	Rose Sprays, litho
8303 to 8305	Gainsborough	Strawberry, litho
8306	Bute	Rose & Violets, litho
8307	Bute	Rose Border, litho
8308	Gainsborough	Cornflower, litho
8309	Violet	Cornflower, litho
8310	Dainty	Roses
8311	Bute	

January 1911

8312	New York	Ivy Design

Appendix E : Earthenware Reference Guide

This appendix lists the earthenware pattern numbers which fall within the Wileman period together with a brief description. It is intended as a quick reference guide.

The information has been compiled from the original pattern books, some of which are in poor condition, and therefore it has not always been possible to provide full details. The shapes identified are those designated for the pattern in the pattern books; this does not necessarily mean that the pattern was only applied to that shape.

3001	Vase	Cherubs with musical instruments
3002	Vase	Ancient galleons
3003	Vase	Irises
3004	Vase	Large leaves and stems
3005	Vase	Flowerheads
3006	Vase	Flower and foliage
3007	Vase	Floral
3008	Vase	Egyptian woman
3009	Ewer/Large Jug	Sinuous leaves and berries
3010	Jug	Deep flower border
3011	Three Panels	"POLLY PUT THE KETTLE ON" "SUKEY TAKE IT OFF AGAIN" "WE'LL ALL HAVE TEA. IT'S ALL BOILED AWAY"
3012	Vase	Vertical panel of yellow flowerheads
3013	Vase	Vertical panel of yellow & blue flowers
3014	Vase	Large peony flowers
3015	Vase	Comical owl and an old man
3016	Vase	Mermaid
3017	Vase	Egyptian man
3018	Moon flask	'Art Nouveau' style women's heads
3019	Vase	Large yellow crocus
3020	Vase	Deep border of yellow open flowers
3021	Pot	Floral
3022	Lidded Vase	Water lilies
3023	Vase	Sinuous leaves and flowers
3024	Vase	Panel of St Cecilia
3025	Vase	Woodland or orchard scene
3026	Handled Bowl	Head & shoulders of young women
3027	Vase	Moulded man's head
3028	Jug (?)	Heads of young women
3029	Vase	Yellow crocus flowers
3030	-	Vertical panel of mauve flowerheads
3031	Jug	Sinuous leaf pattern
3032	-	Sinuously trunked tree
3033	Vase	Large standing bird
3034	Vase	Galleon
3035	Pot	Horizontal border of swimming fish
3036	Jug	Floral
3037	Vase	Abstract leaves & small pink flowers
3038	Vase	Floral
3039	Vase	Inwardly curving pink flowerheads
3040	Vase	Large open flowers in blues
3041	Vase	Horizontal border of pink & red flowers
3042	Vase	Abstract floral design
3043	Vase	Daffodil/narcissus flowers
3044	Pot	Sweet peas
3045	Jug	Yellow flowers
3046	Vase	Tall lilies with drooping flowerheads
3047	Vase	Peacock
3048	Vase	Two peacocks standing back to back
3049	-	See 3084. (No further details)
3050	Jug	Deep border of bluebells
3051	Jug	Tall yellow flowers
3052	Coffee Pot	Dragon
3053	Oriental Coffee Pot	Swans

135

Number	Item	Description
3054	Lidded Square Pot	Large blue flowers
3055	Lidded Pot	Bluebells
3056	Vase	Vertical panel of storks (Rd 330299)
3057	Vase	Tree and flowers
3058	Flowerpot	Large yellow flowers
3059	Flowerpot	Stylised floral design
3060	Flowerpot	Fish
3061	Flowerpot	Floral
3062	Flowerpot	Blue flowers
3063	Vase	Pink bell flowers
3064	Bowl	Large yellow flowers
3065	Bowl	Yellow flowers. Inside as the outside
3066A	14" Plaque	Two women sitting on a stone bench
3066B	14" Plaque	Two women sitting on the grass
3067	12" Plaque	Large sunflowers amid foliage
3068	12" Plaque	Head and shoulders of a woman
3069	10" Plaque	Rats
3070	8" Plaque	Young lady awakening in bed
3071	6" Plaque	Moonlight scene
3072	Double necked pot	Stylised floral pattern
3073	Loving Cup	Large mauve flowers
3074	Jug	Mauve flowers
3075	Covered Pot	Large blue flowers with green leaves
3076	Moulded Jug	Face on a bulbous body on 3 feet
3077	Pig Grotesque	
3078	Dragon Grotesque	
3079	Trinket Set	Floral
3080	Monkey Grotesque	
3081	Oriental Teapot	Two horizontal borders of flowers
3082	Toad Grotesque	
3083	Vase	Red tulips
3084	Vase	Panel of geese
3085	Letter Rack	Yellow & mauve flowers with foliage
3086	Vase	Large yellow sunflowers
3087	Elephant	
3088	Inkpot	Abstract flowing leaf design
3089	Round Inkpot	Yellow flower; blue bird with letter
3090	Inkpot Stand	Two cherubs; blue bird with letter
3091	Candlestick	Heart designs
3092	Lidded Container	Stylised peacock
3093	Lidded Container	Stylised peacock and foliage
3094	Moon Flask	Large sunflowers
3095	24" Vase	Herons
3096	Dragon Grotesque	
3097	-	Not used
3098	Owl Grotesque	
3099	Gryphon Grotesque	
3100	Handled Bowl	Large daffodils
3101	Handled Bowl	Large purple flowers
3102	Handled Bowl	Large sunflowers
3103	Vase	Blue flowers
3104	Plaque (?)	Peacock design (?). Unfinished
3105	John Bull Jug	
3106	Tile	Large pink and red flowers
3107	Vase	Large yellow sunflowers
3108	Vase	Stylised blue flower and foliage
3109	Vase	Stylised floral and leaf design
3110	Vase	Large swan on a blue background
3111	Vase	Large pink roses
3112	Candlestick	Stylised heart/leaf design
3113	Candlestick	Large yellow flowers
3114	Candlestick	Large yellow flower
3115	Small Clock	"Time and Tide Wait For No Man"
3116	Clock	"Prithee Whats O'Clock"
3117	Three-Legged Ringtailed Pig	
3118	Umbrella Stand	Panels of yellow flowers
3119	Pedestal	Vertical panels of stylised flowers
3120	Rococo Flowerpot	(Small size). Large pansies
3121	Rococo Flowerpot	(Medium size). Large yellow flowers
3122	Rococo Flowerpot	(Large size). Owls standing
3123	Tile	No details
3124 A	Tiles	Pair with women's heads as 3028
3124 B		Head with crown
3125 A	Tiles	Head with helmet
3125 B		Pair with women's heads as 3018
		Head with roses
		Head with lilies
3126	Tile	Woman's head as 3068
3127	Tile	Anemones as 3021

136

3128	Tile	"Scales on leaf"	
3129	Tile	"Three Poppies"	
3130	Tile	Repeating heart flower	
3131	Tile	Bluebell	
3132	Tile	Geese panel	
3133	Tile	Grapes	
3134	Baby Jug		
3135	Large Lidded Jar	Panel of rabbits	
3136	Small Covered Jar	Central panel - cats on tree branches	
3137	Covered Pot	Queen Of Hearts	
3138	Monk Jug	Coloured in bronze green	
3139	14" Plaque	No details	
3140	12" Plaque	No details	
3141	10" Plaque	No details	
3142	8" Plaque	No details	
3143	8" Flowerpot	Geese panel	
3144	7" Flowerpot	Geese panel	
3145	6" Flowerpot	Geese panel	
3146	5" Flowerpot	Geese panel	
3147	4" Flowerpot	Geese panel	
3148	8" Flowerpot	Jonquils	
3149	7" Flowerpot	Jonquils	
3150	6" Flowerpot	Jonquils	
3151	5" Flowerpot	Jonquils	
3152	4" Flowerpot	Jonquils	
3153	Vase	Central panel of ducklings	
3154	Square Jug	Monks with jugs of ale	
3155	Umbrella Stand	Herons	
3156	Plain Pedestal	Herons, as 3155	
3157	Umbrella Stand	As 3118 but different border	
3158	14" Plaque	As 3066 with centre as 3068	
3159	Vase	Swans	
3160	Large Clock	Panels of young women	
3161	Plain Pot	Waterlilies and foliage	
3162	Loving Cup & Cover	As 3026	
3163	8" Rose Bowl & Cover	Large yellow flowers	
3164	Vase	Large yellow flowers	
3165	Vase	Geese panel	
3166	Flowerpot & Pedestal	Herons	
3167	Rose Bowl	Game cocks	
3168	Teapots	Jonquils	
3169	Vase	Swimming fish	
3170	8" Plain Pot	Fish	
3171	7" Plain Pot	Fish	
3172	6" Plain Pot	Fish	
3173	5" Plain Pot	Fish	
3174	4" Plain Pot	Fish	
3175	Jugs	Jonquils. Matches teapots 3168	
3176	Triplet Flower Pot	Swimming fish	
3177	Teapots	Japan	
3178	Jugs	Japan. To match 3177	
3179	Rose Bowl	(Large size). Geese	
3180	Rose Bowl	(Medium size). Geese	
3181	Rose Bowl	(Small Size). Geese	
3182	Candlestick	Silver. (No details)	
3183	Imperial Teapot	Representation of a crown	
3184	Chippendale Teapot	No details	
3185	Toilet.	Japan, as 3177; pink effect	
3186	Toilet.	Japan, as 3177; green effect	
3187	Toilet.	Japan, as 3177; yellow effec.	
3188	Triplet Pot.	Jonquils	
3189	Flowerpot	(Large) to match pedestal with Geese	
3190	Flowerpot	(Small) to match pedestal with Hares	
3191	Pedestal	(Large). Geese design	
3192	Pedestal	(Small). Hares design	
3193	Flowerpot	(Small). Geese design	
3194	Pedestal	(Small). Geese design	
3195	Flowerpots	(5 Sizes). Large flowers	
3196	Flowerpots	(5 Sizes). As 3195, green colourway	
3197	Flowerpots	(5 Sizes). As 3195, yellow colourway	
3198	Vase	As 3002, done in greens	
3199	Vase	As 3012, done in greens	
3200	Vase	As 3023, done in greens	
3201	Flask	As 3028, done in greens	
3202	Vase	As 3030, done in greens	
3203	Vase	As 3033, done in greens	
3204	Vase	As 3034, done in greens	
3205	Vase	As 3036, done in greens	
3206	Vase	As 3039, done in greens	

3207	Vase	As 3041, done in greens	
3208	Vase	As 3042, done in greens	
3209	Vase	As 3044, done in greens	
3210	Coffeepot	As 3053, done in greens	
3211	Flowerpot	As 3058, done in greens	
3212	Flowerpot	As 3059, done in greens	
3213	Flowerpot	As 3060, done in greens	
3214	Flowerpot	As 3061, done in greens	
3215	Flowerpot	As 3062, done in greens	
3216	Bowl	As 3064, done in greens	
3217	Jug	As 3074, done in greens	
3218	Lidded Pot	As 3075, done in greens	
3219	-	As 3107, done in greens	
3220	-	As 3108, done in greens	
3221	-	As 3109, done in greens	
3222	-	As 3137, done in greens	
3223	-	As 3118, done in greens	
3224	-	As 3119, done in greens	
3225	Flowerpot	To match 3224	
3226	-	As 3156, done in greens	
3227	-	As 3161, done in greens	
3228	Flowerpot	decorated as 3058	
3229	Flowerpot	As 3059 but red background	
3230	-	As 3021, done in greens	
3231	-	As 3176, done in greens	
3232	-	As 3115, done in greens	
3233	-	As 3056, done in greens	
3234	3.5" Flowerpot	Geese	
3235	3" Flowerpot	Geese	
3236	Salads	Japan. Pink	
3237	Cheese Stand	Japan. Pink	
3238	Trinket Set	Japan. Pink	
3239	Trinket Set	Japan. Green	
3240	Trinket Set	Japan. Yellow	
3241	Dainty Egg Frame	Japan. Pink	
3242	Dainty Muffin	Japan. Pink	
3243	Dainty Butter	Covered on Stand. Japan. Pink	
3244	Dainty Muffin	Covered. Japan. Pink	
3245	Dainty Triplet Tray		
3246	Kruger Teapot	Japan. Pink	
3247	Teapot Stand	Japan. Pink	
3248	Plain Shape Lamp	Green Storks	
3249	Grecian Lamp	Green Anemones	
3250	Grecian Lamp	Jonquils	
3251	Grecian Lamp	Fish	
3252	Plain Shape Lamp	Swans	
3253	Round Fern Box	Green Buttercups	
3254	Round Fern Box	Geese	
3255	Round Fern Box	Cats amongst blossom branches	
3256	Plain Shape Lamp	Japan. Green	
3257	Plain Shape Lamp	Japan. Yellow	
3258	Grecian Lamp	Japan. Pink	
3259	Grecian Lamp	Geese	
3260	Tea Kettle	Plain Shape. Japan. Pink	
3261	Dainty Muffin	Covered (Small size). Japan. Pink	
3262	Tobacco Jar	Ducklings	
3263	Tobacco Jar	Anemones, done in greens	
3264	Tobacco Jar	Cats amongst blossom branches	
3265	Tobacco Jar	Geese	
3266	Toilet Set	Storks, done in greens	
3267	Toilet Set	Anemones, done in greens	
3268	Drinking Horns	No details	
3269	Mug	No details	
3270	Match-striker	No detail	
3271	Biscuit Jar	Anemones, done in greens	
3272	Salad Bowl & Server Handles	Buttercups, done in greens	
3273	Salad	Japan. Pink	
3274	Biscuit Jar	Japan. Pink	
3275	Salad	Japan. Yellow	
3276	Biscuit Jar	Japan. Yellow	
3277	Salad	Japan. Green	
3278	Biscuit Jar	Japan. Green	
3279	Vase	Farmyard design	
3280	Lidded Vase/Jar	Panel of turkeys	
3281	Vase	Farmyard design	
3282	Tobacco Jar	Three old men, drinking and smoking	
3283	Vase	Two panels of swimming fish	
3284	Vase	Fish	

No.	Item	Description
3285	Vase	Fish
3286	Square Box	Flowers, done in greens
3287	Fern Box	Farmyard Scene
3288	Square Fern Box	As 3286 without cover. Farmyard Scene
3289	Cruet Set	Anemones, done in greens
3290	Cruet Set	Japan. Pink
3291	Salad	Hares
3292	Plain Biscuit Box	Geese
3292A	-	As 3292 with additional orange band
3293	Salad	Geese
3294	Biscuit Box	Hares
3294A	-	As 3294 but hares in pale brown
3295	Cruet Set	As 3289 but with earthenware covers
3296	Cruet Set	As 3290 but with earthenware covers
3297	Jug	Farmyard Scene
3298	Vase	Farmyard Scene
3299	Cruet Set	(Cancelled)
3300	Cruet Set	(Cancelled)
3301	Square Box & Cover	As 3286
3302	Salad & Biscuit Jar	Japan. Green. For Mounting
3303	Salad & Biscuit Jar	Japan. Yellow effect. For Mounting
3304	Trinket Set	As 3079, done in greens
3305	Fern Box	Jonquils
3306	Kettle	Jonquils
3307	Biscuit Jar	Large Irises
3307A	-	As 3307 but all leaves done in green
3308	Biscuit Jar	Farmyard Scene
3309	Biscuit Jar	Three men smoking
3310	Roman Toilet	No details
3311	Cat	Blue and yellow; Fleur de Lys design
3312	Cat	Yellow with green leaves all over
3313	Cat	Green with ten rats scattered over
3314	Kings Shape Toilet	No detail
3315	Barrel Biscuit Jar	No detail
3316	Small Honey Pot	No detail
3317	Plain Shape Teapot	Hares
3318	Plain Shape Teapot	Ducklings
3319	Plain Shape Teapot	Farmyard Fowl
3320	Flowerpot	Small to match pedestal. Hares
3321	Small Cat	As 3311
3322	Small Cat	As 3313.
3323	Tobacco Jar	Yellow buttercups, done in greens
3324	Small Cat	Farmyard Scene
3325	Beer Pull	Japan. Yellow
3326	Beer Pull	Japan. Pink
3327	Beer Pull	Japan. Green
3328	Beer Pull	Anemones
3329	Clock	"Wake Up And Get To Business"
3330	Clock	"The Time O Day"
3331	Clock	"Keep Time"
3332	Tobacco Jar	No detail
3333	Vase	Panel of lambs
3334	Vase	Large flowers
3335	Vase	Large blue flowers
3336	Vase	Woman on a wooden balcony
3337	Tobacco Jar	As 3309, but no border
3338	Small Cat	Decorated as 3312
3339	Vase	Witch on a broomstick; "I'll Luck Fly Away"
3340	Vase	Herald
3341	Tobacco Jar	No details
3342	Three-Handled Mug	(Small size). Three men smoking
3343	Vase	Ladies crossing a bridge
3344	Lidded Bowl	Fish
3345	-	No details
3346	3.5" Flowerpot	Fish
3347	3" Flowerpot	Fish.
3348	3.5" Flowerpot	Jonquils
3349	3" Flowerpot	Jonquils
3350	Three-Handled Mug	(Large size). As 3015; Old Man
3351	Three-Handled Mug	(Large size). Large pink flowers
3352	Vase	Sinuous brown tree with pink fruit
3353	Vase	River flowing under bridge & tree
3354	Vase	Sinuous brown tree with pink fruit
3355	Tobacco Jar	Japan. Green
3356	-	Face of Chamberlain
3357	-	Face of Lord S
3358	-	Face of Sir W Harcourt

No.	Item	Description		No.	Item	Description
3359	-	Face of Lord Balfour		3429 to 3435	Flowerpots	(Decreasing in size from 8" to 3")
3360	-	Face of Lord Rosebery		3436	Vase	Farmyard Scene
3361	-	Face of Sir H Campbell Bannerman		3437	Vase	Farmyard Scene
3362	Trinket Set	As 7187 but in green		3438 to 3448	-	Sprays of pink flowers
3363	Toilet Set	As 3362		3449 to 3453	-	As 3437 on different shapes
3364	-	Not used		3454	Vase	Not done intarsio. No details
3365	6" Flowerpot	As 3362		3455	Clock	Farmyard decoration
3366	5" Flowerpot	As 3362				"The Days May Come The Days
3367	4" Flowerpot	As 3362				May Go"
3368	Bowl	(Small size). As 3167		3456	Teapot	Geese decoration
3369	Long Crinkled Box	Anemones in blue, as 3021		3457	Jug	"What An Intolerable Deal Of Sack
3370	-	As 3169 but blue handles				To Such A Pitiful Proprtion Of Bread"
3371	Square Crinkled Box	As 3021		3458	Tobacco Jar (?)	Man's head smoking a pipe
3372	Coffee Pot	Chamberlain		3459	Scotchman	No detail
3373	Coffee Pot	Lord S		3460	Irishman	No detail
3374	Coffee Pot	Lord Rosebery		3461	Vase	Sailing galleon
3375 to 3377	-	Not Done		3462	Vase	Stylised tree
3378	Vase	Hares		3463	Vase	Red-roofed church (or house)
3379	Vase	Kingfisher		3464	Vase	Turretted castle
3380	Vase	Fruit trees with geese		3465	Vase	Shakespeare subjects
3381	Vase	Deep border rim of jester's heads		3466	Vase/Flask	Shakespeare subjects
3382	Vase	Dutch boy and girl		3467	Vase	Shakespeare subjects
3383	Jug	Royal Crest		3468	Vase	Shakespeare subjects
3384	Vase	Full figures of King and Queen		3469	Vase.	Watermill, bridge and house
3385	Vase	Figure of King only		3470	-	Shakespeare - Ariel & Puck
3386	Vase	As 3385 but Queen replacing King		3471	-	Yorick. (Drawing only)
3387	Vase	Large Irises		3472	Flowerpot	Farmyard Scene
3388	Tazza	Deep panel of swimming fish		3473	-	Not used
3389	-	Geese		3474 to 3480	Flowerpots	(Decreasing in size from 8" to 3")
3390 to 3408	-	No details		3481 to 3483	Bowls	Farmyard Scene
3409A	Bowl	Geese border on inside				(Large, Medium and Small sizes).
3410	-	No details				Farmyard decoration inside
3411	Vase	Red Indians		3484	Vase	Farmyard
3412	Vase	Red Indians		3485	Vase	Farmyard
3413	-	As 3414?		3486	Jug	Farmyard
3414	Vase	Sprays of small flowers		3487	Clock Case	Farmyard
3415 to 3425	Vases	All as 3414		3488	Clock Case	Farmyard
3426	Rosebowl	(Large size). Farmyard scene inside		3489	Clock Case	Farmyard
3427	Rosebowl	(Medium size). Farmyard Scene		3490	Bowl	Farmyard
3428	Rosebowl	(Small size). Farmyard Scene		3491	Vase	Farmyard

3492	Vase	Galleon, as 3461	4008A	Yellow flowers, red centres
3493	Vase	Galleon, as 3461	4008B	Blue flowers, yellow centres
3494	Vase	Farmyard	4009 to 4013	Not used
3495	Clock Case	Farmyard	4014A	Yellow flowers, red centres
3496	Vase	Farmyard	4014B	Blue flowers, yellow centres
3497	Vase	Farmyard	4015 to 4017	Not used
3498	Tulip Biscuit Jar	For mounting. Yorick	4018A	Yellow flowers, red centres
3499	Tulip Biscuit Jar	For mounting. Shakespeare Subjects	4018B	Blue flowers, yellow centres
			4019 to 4020	Not used
3500	Straight Biscuit Jar	For mounting. As 3457, two scenes	4021A	Yellow flowers, red centres
3501	Plate or bowl	Decorated inside. As 3457, two scenes	4021B	Blue flowers, yellow centres
			4022A	Yellow flowers, red centres
3502	Bowl	Shakespeare Subjects	4022B	Blue flowers, yellow centres
3503	Bowl	Yorick	4023A	Yellow flowers, red centres
3504	Bowl	No details	4023B	Blue flowers, yellow centres
3505	Bowl	Much Ado	4024 to 4025	Not used
3506	Bowl	Yorick	4026A	Yellow flowers, red centres
3507	-	As 3501 but for mounting	4206B	Blue flowers, yellow centres
3508	-	As 3502 but for mounting	4207 to 4044	Not used
3509	-	As 3503 but for mounting	4045A	Yellow flowers, red centres
3510	-	As 3504 but for mounting	4045B	Blue flowers, yellow centres
3511	-	As 3505 but for mounting	4046 to 4051	Not used
3512	-	As 3506 but for mounting	4052A	Yellow flowers, red centres
3513	Fern Case	Farmyard as 3474	4052B	Blue flowers, yellow centres
3514	Fern Case	Farmyard	4053A	Yellow flowers, red centres
3515 to 3519	Fern Pots	(Decreasing in size from 7" to 3.5")	4053B	Blue flowers, yellow centres
		Farmyard	4054 to 4055	Not used
3520	-	Not used	4056A	Yellow flowers, red centres
3521	Flowerpot	Farmyard as 3513	4056B	Blue flowers, yellow centres
3522	Bottle Vase	Much Ado	4057A	Yellow flowers, red centres
3523 to 3526	Vases	Farmyard	4057B	Blue flowers, yellow centres
3527	Plain Shape Pot	As 3354 only on 3" pot	4058A	Yellow flowers, red centres
3528	Mug	(Large size). As 3342	4058B	Blue flowers, yellow centres
			4059A	Yellow flowers, red centres
	//———//		4059B	Blue flowers, yellow centres
			4060A	Yellow flowers, red centres
4001 to 4005	-	Not used	4060B	Blue flowers, yellow centres
4006A	-	Yellow flowers, red centres	4061A	Yellow flowers, red centres
4006B	-	Blue flowers, yellow centres	4061B	Blue flowers, yellow centres
4007	-	Not used	4062A	Yellow flowers, red centres

141

4062B	-	Blue flowers, yellow centres	
4063A	-	Yellow flowers, red centres	
4063B	-	Blue flowers, yellow centres	
4064 to 4074	-	Not used	
4075A	-	Yellow flowers, red centres	
4075B	-	Blue flowers, yellow centres	
4076 to 4114	-	Not used	
4115A	-	Yellow flowers, red centres	
4115B	-	Blue flowers, yellow centres	
4116A	-	Yellow flowers, red centres	
4116B	-	Blue flowers, yellow centres	
4117 to 4136	-	Not used	
4137A	-	Yellow flowers, red centres	
4137B	-	Blue flowers, yellow centres	
4138 to 4159	-	Not used	
4160A	-	Yellow flowers, red centres	
4160B	-	Blue flowers, yellow centres	
4161	-	Not used	

———————//

6004	Vase	Cat & Hares	
6005 - 6010	-	Not used	
6011	-	Dog & Fowl	
6012 - 6017	-	Not used	
6018	Moon Flask	Turkey & Rabbits	
6019 - 6020	-	Not used	
6021	Vase	Cockerels & Chicks	
6022	Lidded Vase/Jar	Crowing Cockerel & Fowl	
6023	Vase	As 6011	
6024 - 6031	-	Not used	
6032	Tall Jug	Cat & Gosling	
6033 - 6034	-	Not used	
6035	Vase	Rabbits	
6036	Low Jug	Dogs & Lion	
6037 - 6043	-	Not used	
6044	Vase	Dutch Boy & Swans	
6045	Low Jug	Dog & Fowl	
6046 - 6057	-	Not used	
6058	Flowerpot	(Large); As 6287; Dogs & Cockerels	

6059	Flowerpot	(Medium); As 6058	
6060	Flowerpot	(Small); As 6058	
6061	Flowerpot	(Very Small); As 6060	
6062	Flowerpot	As 6004; Cat & Hares	
6063 - 6106	-	Not used	
6107	Vase	As 6036	
6108	Vase	Frog & Ducklings	
6109	Vase	As 6108	
6110 - 6114	-	Not used	
6115	Clock Case	Dog & Bottle	
6116	Clock Case	Dogs chasing fowl	
6117 - 6135	-	Not used	
6136	Covered Vase/Jar	As 6021	
6137 - 6159	-	Not used	
6160	Clock Case	As 6011	
6161 - 6175	-	Not used	
6176	Triple Flowerpot	As 6160 & 6011	
6177 - 6233	-	Not used	
6234	Flowerpot	Cat with Hare	
6235	Flowerpot	Dogs chasing cockerel	
6236 - 6252	-	Not used	
6253	Flower Trough	As 6272	
6254 - 6270	-	Not used	
6271	Biscuit Jar	Cockerels & Chicks	
6272	Bowl	Dog chasing cockerel	
6273 - 6281	-	Not used	
6282	Tobacco Jar	Cockerel & Chicks	
6283 - 6285	-	Not used	
6286	Square Covered Fern Box	Dogs chasing cockerels	
6287	Flower Trough	As 6116	
6288	Square Fern Box	As 6286	
6295	Cruet Set	Dogs chasing cockerels & hens	
6296 - 6298	-	Not used	
6299	Cruet Set	As 6295 but for mounting	
6300 to 6314	-	Not used	
6315	Biscuit Jar	No details	
6316	Small Honey Pot	No details	

———————//

7002	Large Jug	Floral central border	
7003	Large Jug	Yellow & white/pink flowers	
7004	Dainty Toilet	Pink and ivory; gold finish	
7005	Dainty Toilet	Fawn and grey; gold finish	
7006	Toilet	Crane in flight	
7007	Toilet	Geese panel	
7008	Teapot	Roses in panels; gold finish	
7009	–	Not used	
7010	Dainty Toilet	Clematis in green, pink & purple	
7011	Dainty Toilet	Clematis in orange & pink	
7012	Dainty Toilet	Clematis in pink	
7013	Dainty Toilet	Clematis in blue	
7014	Dainty Toilet	Violets in yellow	
7015	Teapot	Roses, as 7008; different colourway	
7016	–	Not used	
7017	Teapot	Roses, as 7008; different colourway	
7018	Dainty Toilet	Violets; gold finish	
7019	Dainty Toilet	Violets; gold finish	
7020	Roman Toilet	Aerographed & shaded in green	
7021	Roman Toilet	Aerographed & shaded in brown	
7022	Dainty Cheese	Covered Coloured in blues	
7023	Shell Flowerpot	Shaded	
7024	Shell Pedestal		
7025	Triple Tray	Shamrock	
7026	Dainty Triple Tray	Coloured in blues; gold finish	
7027	Dainty Salads	Coloured in blues; gold finish	
7028	Teapot	Floral; gold finish	
7029	Jug	As 7028	
7030	–	Not used	
7031	Jug	Floral; gold finish	
7032	Shell Toilet	Shaded; gold finish	
7033	Teapot	Figures in period dress	
7034	Shell Toilet	Poppies; green shaded background	
7035	Shell Toilet	Poppies; yellow shaded background	
7036	Shell Toilet	Poppies; pink shaded background	
7037	Shell Toilet	Rose garlands, ribbons, rosettes & leaves	
7038	Shell Toilet	As 7037, different colourway	
7039	Vesper Jug	Monks	
7040	Vesper Jug	As 7039 but best gold handle	
7041	Dainty Toilet	Shaded in yellow; gold finish	
7042	Teapot	As 7033, pink ground; gold finish	
7043	Dainty Toilet		
7044	Dainty Toilet		
7045	Dainty Cheese	Yellow Crocus	
7046	Dainty Cheese	Purple Crocus	
7047	Chippendale Toilet	Shaded in pink and green	
7048	Chippendale Toilet	Shaded in grey and fawn	
7049	Dainty Toilet		
7050	New Shape Toilet	Pink	
7051	New Shape Toilet	Blue	
7052	New Shape Toilet	Yellow	
7053 to 7056	New Shape Toilet	Green(s)	
7057	New Shape Toilet	Old Gold	
7058	New Shape Toilet	Urbato Jonquil	
7059	Dainty Toilet	Urbato Crocus	
7060 to 7061	–	Not used	
7062 to 7063	New Square Toilet	Clematis, as 7011	
7064	New Square Toilet	Violets, as 7013	
7065	Dainty Toilet	As 7032 but no gold	
7066	–	As 7054 but brown edge	
7067	–	As 7051 but brown edge	
7068	–	As 7052 but brown edge	
7069	–	As 7010 but brown edge	
7070	Chippendale Toilet	Shaded yellow; gold finish	
7071	New Shape Toilet	As 7050 but brown edge	
7072	Dainty Salads	Three sizes; shaded yellow	
7073	Dainty Salads	Green shaded into pink	
7074	Dainty Salads	Fawn shaded into ivory	
7075	Chippendale Teapot	Three sizes; shaded yellow	
7076	Chippendale Teapot	Fawn shaded into green	
7077	Chippendale Teapot	Green shaded to pink	
7078	Dainty Toilet	Coloured in blues	
7079	Dainty Toilet	Coloured in greens	
7080	Dainty Toilet	Coloured in browns	
7081	Dainty Toilet	Coloured in pinks	
7082	Chippendale Toilet	Shaded in yellow, as 7070; no gold	
7083	Chippendale Toilet	Yellow shaded to green; gold finish	
7084	Chippendale Toilet	Yellow shaded to pink; gold finish	
7085	Chippendale Toilet	Green shaded to yellow; gold finish	

No.	Shape	Description		No.	Shape	Description
7086	Foley Toilet			7145	Roman Toilet	As 7144; red ground
7087 to 7108	-	Missing entries		7146	Roman Toilet	As 7144; brown ground
7109	Dainty Plain	As 7083; no gold		7147	Roman Toilet	As 7144; green ground
7110	Plain Toilet			7148	Roman Toilet	Tapestry in green
7111	Chippendale Toilet			7149	Roman Toilet	Tapestry in red
7112	Foley Toilet			7150	Roman Toilet	Carnation in pink & red
7113	Chippendale Toilets			7151 to 7152	Roman Toilet	Carnation, different colourways
7114 to 7117	Dainty Toilet			7153	Roman Toilet	Roses & Fleur de Lys; green ground
7118	Chippendale Toilet			7154	Roman Toilet	As 7153; pink ground
7119	Imperial Toilet	Roses on blue ground; gold finish		7155	Roman Toilet	As 7153; green ground
7120	Chippendale Toilet	Small Daisy; green & brown ground; gold finish		7156	Roman Toilet	As 7153; yellow ground
7121	Chippendale Toilet	Large Daisy; green ground; gold finish		7157	Roman	Tulip in greens; gold finish
7122	Chippendale Toilet	Wisteria; blue ground; gold finish		7158	Roman	Tulip in blues; gold finish
7123	Dainty Toilet	As 7005; no gold		7159	Roman	Tulip in reds; gold finish
7124	Toilet	Yellow Crocus; red background		7165	Kings	Tulip; different colourways
7125	Toilet	Yellow Crocus; blue background		7166 to 7167	Chippendale	Yellow ground
7126	Foley Toilet	As 7101; solid yellow ground		7168	Tobacco Jar	Golf Subject
7127	Dainty Toilet	Shaded green		7169 to 7171	Roman	Solid colours
7128	Toilet	Grey & pink Crocus; yellow ground		7172	Foley Toilet	As 7105 but red
7129	Chippendale Toilet	Roses; yellow ground; gold finish		7173	Foley Toilet	
7130	Imperial Toilet	Pink roses; green ground; gold finish		7174	Tobacco Jar	Delft shaded yellow
7131				7175	Tobacco Jar	Delft shaded blue
7132	Dainty Toilet	Poppies on green ground; gold finish		7176 to 7178	Tobacco Jars	Plain Shape; blue ground; motto
7133	Chippendale	Wild Duck; pink ground; gold finish		7179	Imperial Toilet	Yellow ground
7134	Chippendale	Roses; green ground; gold finish		**December 1901**		
7135	Dainty	Iris; grey ground; gold finish		7180	-	As 7145; different colourway
7136	Imperial Toilet	Birds on branches		7181	-	As 7151; different colourway
7137	Imperial Toilet	Quails; gold finish		7182	-	As 7149; different colourway
7138	Imperial Toilet	Clematis; gold finish		7183	-	As 7125; different colourway
7139	Foley Toilet	As 7101, special order for Cole Bros		7184	-	As 7105 & 7172; different colourway
7140	Foley Toilet	As 7125; red ground		7185	-	As 7160; different colourway
7141	Chippendale Toilet	As 7084 but pink base		7186	-	As 7144; different colourway
7142	Chippendale Toilet	As 7141 but gold as 7032		7187	-	As 7161; different colourway
7143	Toilet	Rose spray; green ground		7188	-	As 7108; different colourway
7144	Roman Toilet	Honesty; mother-of-pearl; blue ground		7189	-	As 7126; different colourway
				7190	-	As 7136; different colourway

No.	Shape	Description
7191	Toilet	Stylised floral & foliage
7192	Toilet	Tulips
7193 to 7194	-	As 7192; different colourways
7195	Roman	Irises in blue & purple
7196 to 7197	-	As 7195; different colourways
7198	Chippendale Toilet	Maids Of Lea (or Sea or Teal)
7199	Shell Flowerpot	No pedestal; green; vellum centre
7200	Shell Pedestal	Green; vellum centre
7201	Dainty Toilet	Pink & green
7202 to 7204	Foley Toilets	Iris
7205 to 7207	Roman Toilets	Iris
7208	Imperial Toilet	As 7191; different colourway
7209	Foley Toilet	solid greens
7210 to 7212	Foley Toilets	As 7209; different colourways
7213 to 7214	Imperial Toilets	As 7191; different colourways
7215	Roman Toilet	As 7148; different colourway
7216	Chippendale Toilet	As 7037; different colourway
7217	12" Dainty Salad	Green shaded into pink; gold finish
7218	Chippendale Toilet	Small Roses; gold finish
7219	Vegetable Dish	Bourbon Spray; As China 7070; gold
7220	10" Bacon Dish	As 7219; gold finish
7221	Asparagus Dish	As 7219; gold finish
7222	Chippendale Toilet	Roses in pink & purple; gold finish
7223	Chippendale Toilet	Festoon of Roses; trinket sets to match
7224	-	As 7223 but gold finish
7225	New York Teapot	Floral spray & leaves
7226	New York Teapot	As 7225; different colourway
7227	New York Teapot	Festoon of Roses
7228	New York Teapot	Persian Iris
7229 to 7230	New York Teapots	Persian Iris; different colourways
7231	Chippendale Toilet	As 7222 but no gold
7232	Tankard Jugs	To match 7225
7233	Tankard Jugs	To match 7226
7234	Tankard Jugs	To match 7227
7235	Tankard Jugs	To match 7228
7236	Tankard Jugs	To match 7229
7237	Tankard Jugs	To match 7230
7238	Tankard Jugs	As 7235 but blue
7239	New York Teapots	As 7228 but blue
7240	Tobacco Jar	Irishman, Scotchman & John Bull
7240A	Tobacco Jar	Frockcoated gentleman
7241	Chippendale Toilet	As 7038 but no gold
7242	Chippendale Toilet	As 7247 (given two numbers in error)
7243	Chippendale Toilet	As 7222 but liquid gold edge
7244	Chippendale Toilet	As 7070 but liquid gold edge
7245	Chippendale Toilet	As 7032 but liquid gold edge
7246	Chippendale Toilet	As 7117, ewer done to match basin
7247	Chippendale Toilet	As 7037; different colourway
7248	Tobacco Jar	Festoons and roses
7249	12" Dainty Salad	Green shaded into pink; gold finish
7250	Chippendale Toilet	As 7152; no gold
7251	Roman Toilet	As 7205 but yellow flowers
7252	Spiral Teapot	Japan

June 1903

No.	Shape	Description
7253	Shallow Beakers	Badged for various confectioners
7254	Jugs	Badged
7255	Tankard Jugs	(Large, Medium & Small); Bourbon Spray (8" & 10"); Bourbon Spray
7256	Bacon Dish	Large floral design; gold finish
7257	Spiral Teapot	As 7257; different colourway
7258	Spiral Teapot	Small flowers in sprays; gold finish
7259	Spiral Teapot	Blue
7260	Kings Toilet	Ivy Leaf Border; garland of roses
7261	Flowerpots	(5 sizes : 8" - 4"); Birds; green ground
7262	Pelican Flowerpot	(5 sizes : 8" - 4"); Birds; yellow ground
7263	Pelican Flowerpots	As 7196 but with red edge
7264	-	Iris
7265	Chippendale Toilet	Red tomatoes, green leaves; gold
7266	Tomato Dish	

February 1904

No.	Shape	Description
7267	Tankard Jugs	Badge in blue; Army & Navy, London

145

7268	Pelican Flowerpots	(5 sizes : 8" - 4"); As 7262 but in red	
7269	Pelican Flowerpots	As 7268 but in green	
7270	Desk Cheese Stand	(Large & small); Festoon of roses	
7271	Roman Toilet	Sprays of small flowers; gold finish	
7272 - 7276	Roman Toilet	As 7271; different colourways	
7277 - 7278	Desk Cheese Stand	(Large & small); gold enhancements	
7279	Desk Cheese Stand	(Large & small); Delphic	
7280	Pelican Flowerpots	(5 sizes : 8" - 4"); as 7262 but in pink	
7281	Pelican Flowerpots	As 7280; different colourway	
7282	Pelican Flowerpots	(5 sizes : 8" - 4"); as 7263 in green	
7283	Leafage Triple Tray	Finished in gold	
7284	Dainty Toilet	As 7004 but liquid gold finish	
7285	Dainty Toilet	As 7005 but liquid gold finish	
7286	Cheese Dish	Peony; gold finish	
7287	Cheese Dish	As 7286; different colourway	
7288	Bevel Tobacco	Smoker's Heads; green ground	
7288A	Bevel Tobacco	As 7288 but brown ground	
7289	New York Teapots, Tankard Jugs	Persian Iris; gold finish	

August 1904

7290	Dainty Toilet	Ivory shaded to yellow; no gold	
7291	Clock Case	No details	
7292	Barrel Clock Case	No details	
7293	Clock Case	Sunflower	
7294	Clock Case	Goblin	
7295	Pedestal	Yellow, brown & green vellums	
7296	Flowerpot	To match 7295	

May 1905

7297	Foley Toilet	Special order	
7298	Imperial Toilet	Special order	
7299	Roman Toilet	Special order	
7300	Roman Toilet	Special order	
7301	Chippendale Toilet	Special order	
7302	Roman Toilet	Special order	
7303	Vase	Oriental floral design; gold finish	
7304	Moon Flask	Oriental floral design; gold finish	

7305	Vase	Oriental floral design; gold finish
7306	Vase	As 7305
7307	Vase	As 7305
7308	-	Not used
7309	Vase	As 7305
7310	Vase	Oriental floral design; gold finish
7311	Vase	As 7309
7312	Vase	Simple oriental floral design; gold finish
7313	Vase	As 7312
7314	Vase	Oriental floral pattern
7315	Vase	As 7314
7316 - 7320	Flowerpots	(5 sizes : 4" - 8"); as 7314
7321	Reid (?) Jug	Detailed oriental floral design; gold finish
7322 - 7323	Jugs	No details
7324 - 7325	Roman Toilets	As 7271; different colourways
7326 - 7327	Roman Toilets	Carnation; finished in different colours
7328 - 7329	Roman Toilets	Tapestry; finished in different colours
7330	Roman Toilet	Solid yellow
7331	Pelican Pots	(5 sizes : 8" - 4"); Delphic Dawn
7332	Pelican Pots	(5 sizes : 8" - 4"); Delphic Sunset
7332A	Pelican Pots	As 7332; different banding
7333	Pelican Pots, Vases, Clocks	Bronze green with pink panel
7334	-	As 7333, yellow panel
7335	Plain Pots,	As 7333, green panel
7336	Vases, China Vases	Delphic Green
7337	Pelican Pots	Roses; Worcester decoration
7338	Pelican Pots	Worcester decoration
7339	Plain Pot	Honesty
7340	Kings Toilet	Delphic Green
7341	Imperial Toilet	Michaelmas Daisy; green finish
7342	Imperial Toilet	As 7341; different colourway
7343	Imperial Toilet	Iris
7344	Imperial Toilet	As 7343; different colourway
7345	Roman Toilet	Fishing Fleet frieze; green finish

7346	Roman Toilet	Dawn	
7347 - 7348	Kings Toilets	Yellow roses litho	
7349	Roman Toilet	Geese frieze; green finish	
7350	Ideal Toilet	Poppies panel	
7351 - 7353	Ideal Toilets	As 7350; different colourways	
7354 - 7355	Ideal Toilets	Dandelion	
7356	Kings Toilet	Daffodil	
7357	-	Not used	
7358	Chippendale Toilet	Peony	
7359	Kings Toilet	Japanese Stork	
7360 - 7361	Roman Toilets	As 7330; colour variations	
7362	Chippendale Toilet	As 7218, Roses	
7363	Roman Toilet	As 7243, Roses	
April 1906			
7364	Tankard Jugs	Badge "Stockport Union Workhouse"	
7365	Roman Toilet	Green	
August 1906			
7366	Kings Toilet	Litho Roses; gold finish	
7367	Vases	Litho large Roses	
7368	Vases	Peony Intarsio	
7369	New York Teapots, Tankard Jugs	Shamrock border; gold finish; to match china	
7370	Roman Toilet	New shape basin; shaded green	
7371	Vases, Kings Toilet	Hunting Subjects	
7372	Vases etc	Motoring Subjects	
7373	-	Peter Pan	
7374	-	Dickens Subjects	
7375	-	Golf Subjects	
7376	-	Fathers of Empire (Rd 407992)	
7377	-	Devil Subject	
7378	-	Smoking Subject	
7379	New Dainty	Litho floral sprays; gold finish	
7380	New Dainty Toilet	Shaded as 7004, in green	
7381	Dainty Toilet	Shaded as 7004, in grey	
7382	New York Teapots	Stork; gold finish	
7383	May Toilet	White body; Festoons; gold finish	
7384	May Toilet	Ivory body; Carnation	
7385	George Toilet	White body; leaf motifs & small festoons	
7386	George Toilet	As 7385; colour variation	
7387	George Toilet	Victorian decoration; gold finish	
1907			
7388	May Toilet	Ivory body; Carnation	
7389	Alexander Toilet	White body; Jewel decoration	
7390	Alexander ToiletI	vory body; scattered pink roses	
7391	Edward Toilet	White body; wreath, ribbon & roses; gold	
7392	Edward Toilet	White body; Honesty	
7393	Marquerite F/Pots	Pink flowers	
7394	Marquerite F/Pots	Yellow flowers	
7395	Marquerite F/Pots	Blue flowers	
7396	-	Litho Conventional Violets	
7397	Vase	Litho Violet Sprays	
7398	Flowerpot	Peony	
7399	Cucumber Tray	Honesty	
7400	Cucumber Tray	Pink flowers; green background	
7401	Desk Cheese Stand	As 7400, yellow flowers	
7402	Vase	Gold enhancements	
7403	New York Teapots, Tankard Jugs	Detailed Japan pattern; gold finish	
7404	New York Teapots, Tankard Jugs	Border pattern with pink roses	
7405	New York Teapots, Tankard Jugs	Pink Rose Wreath	
7406	New York Teapots, Tankard Jugs	Long horizontal wreaths pink roses	
7407	New York Teapots, Tankard Jugs	Leaf design with panels	
7408	Spiral Teapot, Jugs	As 7407	
7409	Plain Bread Tray	As 7406	
7410	Bread Trays	Jewel design	
7411	Edward Toilet	Honesty	
7412	Roman Toilet	Tapestry	
7413	Chippendale Toilet	As 7386	
7414	Candlestick	Rose, Pansy & Forget-me-not; gold finish	
7415	Candlestick	As 7414 but no dontel edge	

147

No.	Item	Description
7416	Vases	Thunderstorm
7417	May Toilet	Wreath with drop roses
7418	Alexander Toilet	Medallion
7419	Alexander Toilet Roses	
7420	George Toilet	Wreath with dropping rose
7421	Edward Toilet	Vine leaves with grapes
7422	Queens Toilet	Festoon of pink roses
7423	Queens Toilet	Pink flowers, green leaves & stems
7424	May Toilet	Cottage with smoking chimney (Pastello)
7425	Vase	Noonday
7426	Vase	Iris (Tristo Ware?)
7427	Flowerpot	Honesty, as 7399
7428	Flowerpot	Honesty, as 7399
7429	Marquerite F/Pot	White and gold
7430	American Jug	Monks after fishing
7431	Cambridge Jugs	Shakespeare Subjects : Merry Wives
7432	Jugs	Monks fishing
7433	Queens Toilet	Medallions with wreath
7434	Queens Toilet	As 7390 with roses
7435	Empress Teapot	Wreath and dropping rose
7436	Kings Toilet	Green
7437	Victoria Teapot	Vine with grapes
7438	Pelican Pots	Fishing scenes
7439	Queens Toilet	Trailing vine with grapes
7440	Roman Toilet	Tapestry
7441	Biscuit, Salad	Dog-Roses on branches, parrot
7442	Biscuit, Salad	Large Carnations; gold finish
7443	Biscuit, Salad	Cranes in green
7444	Biscuit, Salad	Large vines with grapes
7445	Biscuit, Salad	Carnation
7446	Biscuit, Salad	Medallion
7447	Biscuit, Salad	Monks returning from fishing
7448	Biscuit, Salad	Gold printed design
7449	Roman Toilet	Floral
7450	Alexandra Toilet	As 7390
7451	Spiral Teapot	Festoon of pink roses; gold finish
7452	New Spiral Pot	Carnation; gold finish
7453	Vases	Gold Stork print on purple ground
7454	Vases	New Hunting Scenes; gold finish
7455	Roman Toilet	Pink
7456	Vases	Shaded colours
7457	New Flowerpot	Carnation
7458	Chippendale Toilet	As 7366, litho; no gold
7459	-	Golden Morning
7460	Vases etc	Vine; pearl lustre; gold finish
7461	Victoria Teapot	Parrot on branch with Dog-Roses
7462	Victoria Teapot	As 7461; white body
7463	Desk Cheese Stand	As teapot 7451
7464	3-Handled Pint Mug	White body; Vine; gold finish
7465	2-Handled Pint Mug	White body; Vine; gold finish
7466	Victoria Teapot	4 gold lines; gold finish

January 1909

No.	Item	Description
7467	2-Handled Pint Mug	As teapot 7451
7468	Hors d'oevres	Poppy Sprays; gold finish
7469	Dainty Handled Tray	Poppy Sprays; gold finish
7470	Roseberry Oval Tray	Poppy Sprays; gold finish
7471	Roseberry Sq Tray	Poppy Sprays; gold finish
7472	Rococo Oval Tray	Poppy Sprays; gold finish
7473	Rococo Sq Tray	Poppy Sprays; gold finish
7474	Acanthus Oval Tray	Poppy Sprays; gold finish
7475	Acanthus Round	Poppy Sprays; gold finish
7476	New Rococo Tray	Poppy Sprays; gold finish
7477	Ideal Tray	Poppy Sprays; gold finish
7478	Dainty Salad Bowl	Poppy Sprays; gold finish
7479	New Flowerpot	As 7422 with festoon of roses
7480	Biscuit Jar	Litho Rose Spray; gold finish
7481	Biscuit Jar	
7482	Biscuit Jar	Poppy Sprays; gold finish
7483	Biscuit Jar	Poppy Sprays; gold finish
7484	Biscuit Jar	Anemone Sprays
7485	Acanthus Oval Tray	Poppy Sprays; gold finish
7486	Spiral Teapot	Japan
7487 - 7491	Milk Pans/Pails	Various banded decorations
7492	Empress Teapot	White and gold
7493	Empress Teapot	Poppy; gold finish
7494	Empress Teapot	Poppy; gold finish
7495	Desk Cheese Stand	Poppy; gold finish

7496	Cucumber Tray	Shaded in yellow, vellum & brown; gold	7530	Biscuit Jar	Large Peony
7497	Pelican Pots	Poppy; gold finish	7531	Biscuit Jar	Small floral motif
7498	Dainty Duplex Tray	Poppy; gold finish	7532	Victoria Teapot	Poppy; Worcester ground; gold finish
7499	Dainty Tray	Litho Roses; gold finish	7533	4" Plain Flowerpot	Rush decoration, pink & blue flowers
7500	Roseberry Oval	Litho Roses; Worcester decoration; gold	7534	5" Plain Flowerpot	Rush decoration; yellow flowers
7501	Roseberry Square	Litho Roses; Worcester ground; gold	7535	6" Plain Flowerpot	Rush decoration; pink flowers
			7536	Pelican Pot	Litho Roses, as 7337
7502	Acanthus Oval	Litho Roses; blue ground; gold finish	7537	Tobacco Jar	Poppy; Worcester ground; gold finish
7503	Acanthus Round	Litho Roses; Worcester ground; gold	7538	Rococo Sq Tray	Poppy; gold finish
7504	Ideal Tray	Litho Roses; Worcester ground; gold	7539	Biscuit Jar	Anemones; Worcester ground; gold
7505	Hors d'oeuvre	Litho Roses; Worcester ground; gold	7540	Biscuit Jar	As 7539
7506	Triple Tray	Litho Roses; Worcester ground; gold	7541	Biscuit Jar	Carnation Sprays; gold finish
7507	Duplex Tray	Litho Roses; Worcester ground; gold	7542	Biscuit Jar	Vine
7508	Cheese Stand	As 7503	7543	Rococo Oval Tray	Poppy; Worcester ground; gold finish
7509	Pelican Pots	As 7503			
7510	Victoria Teapots	As 7503	7544	Acanthus Round	Poppy; Worcester ground; gold finish
7511	Victoria Jugs	As 7503			
7512	Toast Racks	(5 and 3 bars); As 7503	7545	Acanthus Oval	As 7544
7513	Bread Tray	As 7503	7546	Rococo Round	As 7544 with 4 solid blue panels
7514	Gainsborough Salad	As 7503	7547	Ideal Round	As 7544 with blue embossments
7515	Cress Tray	As 7503	7548	Rococo Square	As 7544 with blue embossments
7516	Celery Tray	Poppy; Worcester ground; gold finish	7549	Dainty Triple Tray	As 7544 with blue embossments
			7550	Biscuit Jar	Litho Roses; Worcester ground; gold
7517	Tomato Tray	As 7503			
7518	Chippendale Toilet	As 7503	7551	Tobacco Jar	Poppy; Worcester ground; gold finish
7519	Honey/Marmalade	As 7503			
7520	Bevel Tobacco Jar	As 7516	7552	-	Laurel; pearl lustre
7521	Tobacco Jar	Spring & Poppy; Worcester ground; gold	7553	-	Pearl lustre
			7554	Old Vase	Figures; pearl lustre
7522	2-Handled Mug	As 7503	7555	Old Vase	Vine & Laurel pearl lustre
7523	2-Handled Goblet	As 7503	7556	-	Cornflower; pearl lustre
7524	New Flowerpot	Medallion	7557	Old Vase	Rabbit Dogs & Rabbits; yellow lustre
7525	Biscuit Jar	Early English; Japan; gold finish			
7526	Biscuit Jar	Gold Stork; pink & blue ground; gold	7558	Biscuit Jar	Poppy; Worcester ground; gold finish
7527	Biscuit Jar	Cornflower; pearl lustre	7559	Biscuit Jar	Litho Roses; Worcester ground; gold
7528	Biscuit Jar	Laurel; pearl lustre			
7529	Biscuit Jar	Iris			

No.	Item	Description
7560	Vase	Bird View; pearl lustre
7561	-	Dragon; pearl lustre
7562	Biscuit	Medallion
7563	Biscuit Jar	Iris; gold finish
7564	Biscuit Jar	Laurel Wreath & Cornflower; gold finish
7565	Biscuit Jar	Red Japan, as 4253; gold finish
7566	Biscuit Jar	Blue Iris
7567	Biscuit Jar	Border of large roses; gold finish
7568	Biscuit Jar	Oriental floral, as china 6888; gold finish
7569	Biscuit Box, Salad	Yellow Iris; see 7529-7566
7570	New York Jugs	Storks & clouds; gold finish; as 7382
7571	New York Jugs	As china 7907; bows & festoons
7572	Vases, Clock Cases	Panels of roses & forget-me-nots; gold
7573	Alexandria Toilet	As 7417
7574	Drip Cups	Gold bands and edge
7575	Drip Cups	Thin gold bands and edge
7576	Roman Toilet	Ivory body; shaded pink
7577	Vases	Cornflower; yellow lustre
7578	Vases	Ivory body; Cornflower
7579	-	Crocodile print with silver bands
7580	Roman Toilet	Carnation, as 7327
7581	Biscuit Jar	Litho festoons of roses; gold finish
7582	Biscuit Jar	Litho of rose sprays & greek key; gold
7583	Biscuit Jar	Large spray of roses, fruit & berries; gold
7584	Biscuit Jar	Litho large spray of roses; gold finish
7585	Biscuit Jar	As 7584; colour variation; gold finish
7586	Biscuit Jar	Linked laurel wreaths & roses; gold
7587	Sundries	Rose motif, as china 10397
7588	Kings Toilet	As 7366; colour variation
7589	Plain Pots	As 7399; colour variation
7590	George Toilet	As 7387; colour variation
7591	Vases	Moonlight scenes
7592	Queens Toilet	As 7573
7593	Acanthus Round	Shamrock; gold finish
7594	Vases	Laurel; pearl lustre
7595	Ideal Toilets	Ivory body; as 7355

October 1909

No.	Item	Description
7596	Chippendale Toilet	White body; shaded in pink; gold finish
7597	Victoria Jug	Crocodile print; badged; silver finish
7598	Kings Toilet	As 7397 but badged
7599	Victoria Teapots	White body; green edge & shoulder line
7600	Biscuit Jar	Pink roses with festoons; gold finish
7601	Biscuit Jar	Anemones; gold finish
7602	Biscuit Jar	Litho flower sprays
7603	Biscuit Jar	Asters; gold finish
7604	Biscuit Jar	Large flowerheads; gold finish
7605	Biscuit Jar	Cats on branches with blossom; gold
7606	Biscuit Jar	Large flowerheads; gold finish
7607	Biscuit Jar	Anemones; gold finish
7607A & B	Biscuit Jars	As 7607; colour variations
7608	Biscuit Jar	Poppy; gold finish
7609	Victoria Jug	Badged; silver finish
7610	Biscuit Jar	Poppy; gold finish
7611	American Jugs	5 scenes; monks fishing & Shakespeare
7612	Roman	Tapestry; ivory body
7613	Pelican Pot	As 7452
7614	2-Handled Salad	(12", 10", 8"); Large flowerheads
7615	2-Handled Salad, Teapots, Jugs, Teapot Stands, Coffee Pots, Covered Jugs	(12", 10", 8"); As 7603, Aster
7616	Victoria Jugs	As 7597, Badged; silver finish
7617	-	As 7615; colour variation

December 1909